The KETO Ice Cream Scoop

52 amazingly delicious ice creams and frozen treats for your low-carb, high-fat life

CARRIE BROWN

with foreword by Brian Williamson
Author, The KETO Diet – A Beginner's Guide

ISBN-10: 1548020664

ISBN-13: 978-1548020668

DEDICATION

Geoff Nyheim

Empowerer of people, celebrator of life, lover of ice cream, and all-round outstanding human being.

Every single day I wake up and thank my lucky stars for the incredible impact you have had on my life. You have had a greater positive influence on me than anyone I have ever known. I have created a life that I love because of your support, your coaching, your encouragement, and your enthusiasm.

You inspire me to do my best work. Your integrity, and the way you are in the world is a constant, shining example to me.

You told me I could do anything I wanted to do...so I did.

CONTENTS

Acknowledgments

Foreword

ACKNOWLEDGMENTS

Brian Williamson – you're my hero. So, there's that. Also, your influence in my life is huge. HUGE. You're my biggest fan, my biggest supporter, and a most splendid podcast cohost. My life is immeasurably better with you in it. You started this whole KETO Ice Cream Cookbook update project, so you have no one to blame but yourself for the deliciousness that resides within.

The Ice Cream Taste Test Crew – Geoff Nyheim, Kati Cole, Deana Fuhriman, Sara Bush, Crystal Mankite, Tina and Danny McManus, Minta Hale, Sahara Pirie, Laurie Resch, Bob Stutz, Jen Meehan, Matt Ballard, and The Bailors (Jonathan, Angela, Mary Rose, and Robert) – whose thoughtful, constructive criticism helped shape many of the final versions. You ate a lot of ice cream during this endeavor, and my recipes are better because of your input.

Marjorie Ferris aka Bea – for delivering a critical bottle of glycerin at just the right moment, and for always being willing to taste just one more flavor.

Bala Silvakumar – you make me look better than any photographer ever has!

Every last one of my lovely blog readers, Facebook groups members, and podcasts listeners – you make this all worthwhile. This book is better because of you, and I am deeply honored and humbled that you choose to be a part of my world.

Mic – MVP, you're the very, very best. That's all.

Marc Levine – you know why.

FOREWORD

When I chose to eat ketogenically, it wasn't difficult to give up the foods that were making me sick, fat, sad, and gross. But the last non-keto food I did finally quit eating was ice cream. That's because I love ice cream.

But I don't just love any ice cream. I'm extraordinarily picky about the content and texture of ice cream. If it's not silky smooth, with a fun flavor profile and/or lots of cool stuff thrown in the mix, I'm not interested. Plain vanilla, when done correctly, is complex. But it's also plain vanilla.

For me, ice cream is packed with way too much potential to settle for anything less than incredible.

Of course, when I go to the grocery store, there are no keto ice cream options available. And that makes me sad. So, the next best option was to try to make some myself. And that was an exercise in frustration. Mostly because the recipes suck. And mostly because people seem willing to settle for less than perfect results.

But that ain't me.

Surely, I have thought for a while now, someone could make a keto ice cream that doesn't suck. Let's face it, ice cream is served up as an ideal keto food. It's full of good fat, remove the sugar and replace it with a natural sweetener, and you'll have a great menu item.

But, alas, I was unable to buy or make any ice cream that lived up to my standards.

And then I tried Carrie's ice cream, when my wife and I visited her in Seattle. And that's when I knew I'd found what I was looking for. Carrie has a the same ridiculously high standards that I do, and she knows how to make things feel and taste like perfection.

And, since you're reading this right now, you will soon know exactly what I mean. The ice cream recipes in this book are, and this is no exaggeration, the greatest food ever conceived of by a human being in the last 200,000 years.

Forget what you know about boring and dull desserts. Forget all previous attempts at horribly bad ice cream.

Read, learn, and enjoy ice cream, the Carrie Brown way. Because she's awesome. And so is her ice cream.

Brian Williamson

Author, The KETO Diet – A Beginner's Guide
www.ketovangelist.com

HOW IT ALL BEGAN

Ice cream, ice cream, we all scream for ice cream!

Ice cream is one of the world's favorite sweet treats. Not mine though. Well, not in the beginning, anyway.

Growing up, my family didn't eat ice cream much. It made a rare, and brief appearance on the Sunday dessert menu every once in a great while, usually in the form of an Arctic Roll. For the uninitiated, an Arctic Roll is a wholly British thing consisting of vanilla ice cream wrapped in a thin layer of sponge cake to form a roll. It's the shape of a log, and there's a layer of raspberry sauce between the ice cream and the sponge. My mother would saw one into 4 and we'd each have a slice. I liked Arctic Roll days, although they didn't roll around very often. Ha ha! Roll. Oh, never mind.

Other than Arctic Rolls, ice cream never really blew my skirt up as a kid. Looking back, I think this was because the ice cream that was available back in the day was so ghastly: thin, almost icy, flavorless. I was well into adulthood when the premium ice creams hit the market, and ice cream was elevated to a whole new status. I would chow down on the odd Ben and Jerry's Cherry Garcia Ice Cream Bar, or sneak a small oblong tub of Mövenpick Café Ice Cream, and boy oh boy, did that stuff make me want to get a room. But still, ice cream was never my go-to dessert or treat.

My personal ice cream ~~fetish~~ odyssey only started some 8 years ago when my neighbor, Larry, decided to have a birthday. His lovely wife, Susan, is not the chef in the family, so I offered to cook The Birthday Dinner for Larry and his family at my home. I had the dinner down, but was somewhat stumped when it came to a suitable dessert. I knew Larry adored raspberries, and I knew the weather was going to be warm; armed only with those two pieces of information I randomly decided that I was going to make Raspberry Ice Cream, even though I had never made ice cream before. Wait. What? A pastry chef that had never made ice cream? Ever? True story. Frankly, ice cream was always a bit of a mystery to me; secretly, the thought of making it was all kinds of discombobulating.

Not being someone who lets scary things stop her from doing anything, I toddled off to Williams-Sonoma to avail myself of an ice cream churner, and my ice cream adventures began. Being a serial overachiever, I made both Raspberry Ice Cream and Raspberry Ripple Ice Cream for Larry's birthday. Huge hits. I mean HUGE. That stuff is homemade? Are you kidding me right now??

That success, combined with the therapeutic experience I had delighted in while making said ice cream, set me off on a path that involved some 40-or-so flavors, and hundreds and hundreds of gallons of ice cream over the next 3 years. What can I say? I am an all-or-nothing kind of girl.

Never one to do things by half, I made ice cream for neighbors, ice cream for friends, ice cream for work colleagues, and ice cream for a local hotel. I rapidly became known as The Ice Cream

Queen. I had strangers gate-crashing work meetings because they heard Carrie Brown's ice cream was making an appearance. Suddenly, getting volunteers for house-painting parties was a breeze. Got ice cream? I'd love to help you paint! It was awesome.

Then I learned what traditional ice cream does to our health, and my whole glorious ice-cream-making nirvana came to a screeching halt.

Unfortunately, traditional ice cream – predominantly made with cow's milk and sugar – is not so good for our health; but despite the health risks, people don't want to give it up – the proliferation of low-fat, fat-free, and dairy-free alternatives are proof of that – and who can blame them? Great ice cream is delicious! Judging by the focus on low-fat, and fat-free ice creams on sale in store freezers across America – and I am sure around the world – you'd be forgiven for thinking that the big, bad ice cream monster is fat. However, scientific research unequivocally shows that the real villain in traditional ice cream is not the fat, it's the sugar.

My education on sugar, and exactly how and why our bodies get fat – not to mention diseased – came from several fantastic sources – starting with Gary Taubes' groundbreaking book, "Why We Get Fat and What To Do About It". That was the catalyst that changed my whole outlook on health and wellness, and I have now dedicated my life to developing recipes that support the findings of Gary's and other fine and brilliant folks' research. I started out by sharing on my blog a few tasty dishes that I rustled up on Friday nights for friends.

Those few tasty dishes blossomed into a fully-fledged food and lifestyle blog, with visitors from all over the world swinging by to get healthy recipes to feed themselves and their families, and to get tips and tricks on following a healthier lifestyle. In some small way, I hope my recipes will help other people reach their health and body-fat goals.

In September 2013, I published my first cookbook, and since then 5 more cookbooks have been written with several more in the works. A KETO food blog was born, a very active Facebook group created, and I partnered up in the studio with the ruggedly handsome Brian Williamson to host a wildly popular health and fitness podcast – Ketovangelist Kitchen – to educate and teach people how to live a truly healthy lifestyle by revolutionizing their adventures in food and cooking. There's also a lot of laughing. *A lot.*

As I created more and more delicious healthy recipes, I decided it had to be possible to create ice creams that taste fantastic – and are indistinguishable from their regular milk-and-sugar-laden cousins – but without compromising our health and body-fat goals.

This book is the result.

My goal was to make ice creams that support our health and body-fat goals, and yet taste as good – or better – than premium regular ice creams. It's a lofty goal if you understand how ice cream works. It's a lofty goal if you've ever been unfortunate enough to try the dairy-free, fat-free, sugar-free, vegan, or whatever-the-heck-free versions at the store. The ice creams in this book won't taste anything like any of those. My trusty Ice Cream Taste Test Crew - and my awesome podcast cohost, Brian - would agree that you cannot tell the difference between the ice creams you'll make using these recipes, and regular premium ice creams.

What I am saying here, lovely people, is that you can, in fact, have it all. You now get to eat fantastic ice cream that will help, not hinder, your health. Even if it was not a search for healthy ice creams that brought you here, why would you eat the regular stuff when you can have a super-healthy option that tastes even better?

These recipes support our health and body-fat goals by providing nutrient dense proteins and fats, as well as being extremely low in carbohydrates, and packed with vitamins and minerals.

All of these recipes are gluten-, grain-, soy-, and sugar-free. All but three of the recipes are egg-free. Many of these recipes are dairy-free, and / or vegan – or can easily be made so with a little tweak.

Every last one of them tastes delicious. Enjoy!

~~~~~~

"I was fortunate enough to be one of Carrie's taste testers for her ice cream recipe development. Keep in mind Carrie and I had never met before this encounter. I've been making regular ice cream for at least a decade myself...so I thought I knew a little about ice cream.

"After only a few bites I was completely stunned at the flavors and textures of these ice creams. I thought, "How could these ice creams be so healthy? No way!"

"So, I asked, the obvious question: "Which ingredients do you use?" and she answered with rapidity I cannot replicate: "If-I-Told-You-I'd-Have-To-Kill-You".

"Now don't get me wrong, Carrie is sweet and generous, make no mistake about it – and when it comes to recipe development she is SERIOUS. I came away from that day with a very happy mouth and satiated belly."

"I am thrilled to see that she has made these recipes available to all of us."

~ Sahara Pirie

AN ICE CREAM FRAME OF MIND

When I first had this harebrained idea to write an ice cream book, the thought seemed rather huge. And a bit daunting. OK, yes. Scary. It was scary. Writing books for other people to read seems so sensible, so grown-up, and so…enormous. Books are supposed to be intelligent, and meaningful, and full of information. And, magical. Books are supposed to be magical. I would get completely lost in story books when I was a young lass growing up in England. These days it's all psychology, cooking, and photography, but books are still magical to me.

Left Brain deftly tried to shoo the whole book idea away, while Right Brain was busy reasoning that I already spend a ton of my time writing stuff for other people to read on my blog anyway, so how was a book so different? Well, that's a bit logical for you, Right Brain.

So, I rattled the ice creamy scheme around my noggin for a bit, and then Right Brain popped up with an entirely convincing argument that really it would be just like writing a whole slew of blog posts, printing them out, and then taping them together down one edge. Of course, a book would be rather neater – not to mention – held together with something other than tape. Anyway, the thing is – as Right Brain so clearly articulated – blog posts aren't the least bit scary.

After all, this whole book thought got started after I innocently posted my recipe for Peanut Butter Ice Cream on my blog one day. In an instant I had a whole cacophony of people clamoring for more healthy ice cream. We want healthy ice cream! We want healthy ice cream!

Once Right Brain had persuaded me that this endeavor was really not so scary, I floated the idea by a few friends, and pinged a few blog and Facebook followers, to a rousing chorus of, "Me! Me! I want the first copy!" Which totally seemed like a sign. So, I followed it.

And here we are, lovely readers far and wide, sitting here, on the brink of embarking on a gloriously delicious adventure together. And I couldn't be happier that Right Brain talked me into it. Because now I get to share with you a way to make your mouths happy and your bodies healthier – all at the same time – and that, is a many-splendored thing.

Once I had determined that a book was indeed going to be written, I planned on dishing up 50 fabulously healthy ice cream recipes along with beautiful images, some (hopefully) exceedingly useful information on ingredients and equipment, and calling it good; except that little voice in my head – I have a suspicion it was Right Brain – kept nagging at me that maybe there was something else that would make it more fun, more readable, more engaging. Heck, just more. I always want to give you lovely readers more.

So, I did a little poll on Facebook asking how much writing you wanted in this book, or whether you just wanted me to give you the recipes already. Turns out the overwhelming majority wanted writing to go with. Who knew? If you're following along with my little blog, or listening to Brian and I on our podcasts, this will all make perfect sense; well, as much as anything that I do makes perfect sense. If you don't know me from a bar of soap however, some of what you read here – in amongst the recipes and decidedly sensible ice-cream-making information – may not make much sense at all, but if there's one thing you should probably know about me, it's that I do like to keep it real. And fun. If we're not having fun here, what's the point?

Left Brain just reminded me that while we're here having fun, we do have a spot of business to attend to. I am chuffed Left Brain piped up; otherwise I'd be skipping off to the Ketovangelist Kitchen to play with sugar-free Chocolate Fudge Sauce that doesn't freeze, or whipping you all up another flavor of ice cream. Some of you may well prefer I go do that. Me too!

BUT…while this book was never intended to get all geeky and scientific in the health and fat-loss department, and even though my recipes don't contain any, I do feel the need to talk for a minute or two about the big, bad ice cream monster: sugar. I want to be sure that you know what you are getting – or not getting – when you chow down on the recipes both in this book, and those over at www.carriebrown.com and www.ketovangelistkitchen.com.

I've noticed that when most recipes say they are sugar-free, what they really mean is they don't have ordinary refined white sugar in them. Typically, the white sugar is replaced by honey, agave, coconut sugar, maple syrup, brown sugar, or increasingly, dried fruits such as dates. What you should be aware of is that our bodies respond to all of these alternatives in essentially the same way that they respond to refined white sugar. For all intents and purposes, sugar is sugar as far as our bodies are concerned, and our bodies cannot tell the difference between refined white sugar and the others I mentioned.

When I say my recipes are sugar-free, I mean they are free of *any added sugars*, or anything that makes your body respond the same way as refined white sugar does. If your goal is fat-loss, you will do far better in reaching that goal with recipes that have neither refined white sugar nor the typically-used alternatives such as those I have mentioned above.

For those of you wondering about fruit, it is true that fruit contains sugar. This is why I only ever use the whole fruit – never juice – and I focus on using the fruits with the least sugar and highest nutritional density: berries and (some) citrus. The fiber in whole fruit helps control the effect of dietary sugar on blood-sugar levels, and our bodies absorb the natural sugars more slowly. We are less likely to experience a spike in our blood sugar levels – such spikes being what we want to avoid. And fiber is good stuff for us, too.

Still, despite the fiber, if fat-loss is your primary goal, you won't want to eat too much fruit-based ice cream at any one time. Luckily, my ice cream recipes are very filling, and I am content with one or two small scoops. When I used to eat regular ice cream I could down a whole pint without even thinking about it. Sugar will do that to you.

Talking of eating ice cream, and notwithstanding how much better for us these ice creams are than traditional ice creams, bear in mind that they should still be considered treats. A body cannot thrive on even the healthiest of ice creams alone. For optimal health and body-fat control, nutrient dense proteins and healthy fats from whole-food sources should form the basis of a ketogenic diet. These ice creams have some protein and are packed with healthy fats. Just eat them as dessert, not the main course!

If you do want all the geeky, scientific info, and detailed research on sugars (and things that our bodies recognize as sugar), I highly recommend you read Gary Taubes' book, "Why We Get Fat and What To Do About It" and Phinney and Volek's book, "The Art and Science of Low Carbohydrate Living". They will explain all you need to know. They changed my life.

Gosh, are you still with me, lovely readers? We're nearly at the fun bits, I promise. I bet you never imagined that ice cream needed so much explaining. But really, if we're going to do this thing, let's do it properly. You never struck me as the types that do things by half. And let me assure you, dear people, once we really get this show on the road, once this train has pulled out of the station, you'll be glad that you persevered through all this typing. Your appreciation for ice cream making will reach new heights and know no bounds! Because ice creams are the single most complex food creations we humans have come up with, and sadly, you cannot just whizz a random bunch of stuff together, churn it, sling it in the freezer and get beautiful, scoop-able, delicious ice cream the next day.

Great ice cream takes planning and preparation, especially in the ingredient and equipment departments. When the time comes to make your first ice cream recipe, you'll thank me for encouraging you to read these sections before you get started. I mean, who wants to have all these glorious recipes for healthy ice cream and then not be able to make them?? Not you.

These next sections detail what you'll need to make your adventures in healthy ice cream making easier and more successful. You could skip over all this technical stuff and dive straight into the recipe section, but understanding how ice creams work will give you the very best chance of getting a fantastic result every time. And I am as certain as I can possibly be that you definitely want fantastic results to fill your eagerly awaiting ice cream bowl with.

So, before you run screaming for joy towards your kitchen to whip up your first batch of fabulously healthy KETO ice cream, I really plead with you to take a few minutes to read the next three (short!) chapters of geeky stuff.

And just one last thing before you move right along. We need to get our brains in an ice cream frame of mind. Because great ice cream takes patience and planning.

<u>Patience</u>

Great ice cream is a process. The {really} good news is that these healthy ice creams are a lot less of a process than regular ice creams. Woohoo! The not-so-good news is that it is still a process. There's lots of waiting involved. Once you've made the base custard you get to wait. Then you churn the ice cream and you get to wait again. Then before you can make another batch you probably need to re-freeze the freezer bowl and you get to wait again. So, you are going to need patience. There will be waiting. If you choose to forego the waiting, you will end up with a not-so-great ice cream, or a dollop of soft-serve. Then you'll be sad. I'll be sad too, because I want the ice cream made from these recipes to be the best ice cream you've ever eaten in your life. I promise you it's totally worth the wait.

Planning

Plan for AT LEAST 24 hours to go by from when you get the blender out to when you'll have a scoop of magnificent ice cream – made by your own fair hands – in your bowl. Two days is even better planning. I typically plan a week in advance, especially if I am making large quantities or a lot of different flavors at once. Yes, I know the box that the ice cream maker came in says you can have frozen treats in 20 minutes, and you can. But don't expect a fantastic scoop of ice cream in a bowl in 20 minutes. They're fibbing. I do believe in telling you how it really is, even if it's not what you really want to hear. My recipes are not recipes for soft-serve. I'll probably get to some of those at some point, but first let's make the real stuff.

When planning, also take into account the time needed to make any mix-ins that you are going to use. Make sure they are ready, and chilled or frozen, before you start churning.

Now really, I'm done jibber-jabbering.

Grab your favorite drink, and settle down in a comfy spot for a few minutes, with a cat if you have one, because cats purring nearby is all kinds of good for us humans.

Then, let the ice cream making begin!

~~~~~~

A few notes from one of my taste-testers, Sara:

Pistachio Rose: *"Other-worldly."*

Sassy Goat: *"All ice creams should be made with goat cheese and mint, in other words, all ice creams should be this ice cream."*

Ballistic Coffee: *"This is the best thing since Turkish coffee."*

Bubblegum Bliss: *"This just makes me happy; it has marshmallows made out of magic."*

INGREDIENTS

I hate to break it to you, but ice cream is complicated. It is the most complicated food concoction we humans have created. It's all science, all the time in Ice Cream Land. There is an awful lot of chemistry involved in getting fat, sugar and water molecules to canoodle into a thick, smooth, creamy, scoop-able relationship when frozen. The good news is that unlike the components of human relationships, their behavior is extremely consistent, and predictable. Maybe that's why I love making ice cream so much. And why I live with 6 5 4 cats (RIP Chiko, Dougal, and Penelope), and no humans.

Fat, sugar, water, and air each critically affect the outcome of ice cream, so it is not as easy as swapping out ingredients ounce for ounce from a traditional ice cream recipe. In order to end up with the right texture and consistency, the fat, water and sugar have to be in exactly the right ratios. If they are not, your ice cream may not freeze sufficiently, or it might freeze like a block of ice and not be scoop-able, or it may end up with an icy graininess and not have the smooth, creamy texture that you love. When it's right though – when you have a great recipe, and follow the instructions – ice cream nirvana shall be yours.

Creating healthy, easy-to-make ice cream means replacing some key traditional ingredients – milk, sugar, and eggs – with others, while keeping the attributes that those key ingredients possess to enable a successful, delicious ice cream.

Once you have the base recipe, every time you add other ingredients to flavor it, you throw the balance of base ingredients off, so compensation must be made to keep it all in balance so that the ice cream still works.

This is even harder to accomplish when you are using ingredients less common in the kitchen. With food manufacturing and labelling what it is these days you can sometimes end up with something you hadn't bargained for. For this reason, I encourage you to use the brands that I do, simply because I know that they work. I am not compensated by any food manufacturers. I just like the products that I use.

A handy link to all the ingredients I use can be found on page 27

This will make purchasing everything you need super-easy and save you a bunch of time and money on figuring out and sourcing what you need. I want your ice cream making adventures to be as easy and joyous as possible!

First I go over the typical base ingredients I use, and then the additional ones used for flavor, texture, and mix-ins.

Base Ingredients

As with any other recipe, the flavor and nutritional quality of ice cream depends to a large extent on the quality of the ingredients used. If you are going to put in the effort to make your own ice cream, I thoroughly recommend using the best ingredients you can get your hands on.

In traditional ice creams, egg yolks are typically one of the main ingredients. Egg yolks are an excellent emulsifier, and impart a smooth and creamy texture to the ice cream custard. The downside to using egg yolks is that you need to master making egg custards. I love making egg custards, but egg custards can be tricky little suckers to get right, and certainly take some time. I wanted to make your ice-cream-making experience as easy and fast as possible, so while eggs are a great addition to a healthy lifestyle, I chose to develop these ice creams without the use of egg yolks, to avoid you having to master making egg custards, and so you get perfect ice cream quicker. I am pretty sure you love the idea of perfect ice cream, quicker. Ice cream that doesn't take 3 months in culinary school to prepare for.

I list here the specific base ingredients that I use for my egg-yolk-less custards, so that you can recreate these ice creams to taste exactly as they were in the Ketovangelist Kitchen. Ice creams generally have very light, subtle flavors, so changes in the base ingredients are more noticeable. Of course, you are free to use different brands, but the finished ice creams will taste slightly different – or a lot different – depending on the brand you use. This is not necessarily a bad thing, I just thought it best to point it out so your expectations are set. I do like to be clear and thorough. Especially when it comes to recipes, choosing paint colors, building kitchen cabinets, and scheduling my next exhilarating road trip adventure.

Coconut Milks

Thick – this is full-fat, very thick, comes in a can, and solidifies in the 'fridge. It is made from coconut meat, and is very high in very healthy fats, especially MCTs (Medium Chain Triglycerides). I won't bore you with the technical details of MCTs – just know that they are extremely good for you. Thick coconut milk helps create a smooth and creamy texture.

Make sure that you buy it unsweetened, and shake the can very well before you open it. If you shake the can and don't hear liquid, stand the can in hot water for 15 minutes to liquefy the contents and then shake vigorously. Thick coconut milk separates in the can. It intended that you use the whole contents, so do not open the can and pour the watery portion away. Shake the can well to mix the watery and the solid parts together before opening.

You can find it in most grocery stores and it is often located with the Asian and / or Indian foods. I used Thai Kitchen Unsweetened Coconut Milk for the recipes in this book.

If you have an intolerance to coconut you can substitute thick coconut milk with heavy cream (see page 12).

Thin – this comes in a carton and is thin like cow's milk, but is very white. It does not become thick when cold. Make sure that you buy it unsweetened. I used Trader Joe's Unsweetened Coconut Milk Beverage for the recipes in this book.

Be sure to use 'thick' or 'thin' coconut milks as noted in the recipe. They are not interchangeable, and it will make a big difference if you don't use the one called for.

If you have an intolerance to coconut you can substitute with almond milk. The taste will be slightly different.

Other Non-Dairy Milks

Hemp – this comes in a carton and is thin like cow's milk, but has a slight caramel color to it. Yes, it is made from hemp seeds which come from the cannabis plant; no, you will not get high off it. Well, if you make fabulous ice cream with it you might, but it won't be the same kind of high.

Make sure that you buy it unsweetened. I used Living Harvest Unsweetened Original Hemp Milk for the recipes in this book. If you can't find hemp milk you can substitute with almond milk. The flavor will be slightly different but it will still work.

Almond – this comes in a carton and is thin like cow's milk, but is darker in color. It is made from soaked almonds, so nut allergy sufferers beware. You can make your own almond milk at home, but honestly, who has time for that? Or the money, come to think of it. I'd rather be making ice cream. Or pottering in the garden. I do love a good potter.

Make sure that you buy it unsweetened. I used Trader Joe's Unsweetened Vanilla Almond Milk for the recipes in this book.

Heavy Cream / Heavy Whipping Cream / Double Cream

I use heavy cream – also known as heavy whipping cream or double cream – in most of my ice cream bases because it imparts a particularly smooth and creamy result, as well as an extra depth of flavor. I do love me a dollop of cream. Heavy cream is a staple of a ketogenic diet.

Look for heavy cream that does not say UHT on the carton. UHT cream has been treated at very high temperatures to give it a long shelf-life, but that heating also destroys the flavor. I never really understood why cream would need a long shelf-life. If it gets as far as my 'fridge, it won't be there on the shelf for long.

I recommend that you use cream that has no added ingredients, and if you can find organic cream, with no hormones or antibiotics, and from grass-fed cows, so much the better.

If you need to make a recipe dairy-free, replace the heavy cream with thick coconut milk. The taste and texture will not be the same, but it will be close. Do NOT replace with thin coconut milk (see page 11 for explanation of thick and thin coconut milks).

Avocado Oil

Avocado oil is a virtually tasteless oil that is pressed from avocados and which is very high in monounsaturated fatty acids. It has an unusually high smoke point, and becomes solid when refrigerated. It is perfect for use in ice creams because it does not impart flavor.

MCT Oil

MCT stands for Medium Chain Triglyceride. MCT Oil is a great source of good fats for energy and helping folks get into ketosis. It is mainly used as an additive to coffee. I use Now brand.

Cheeses and other dairy

Soft cheeses, sour cream, and crème fraiche are also used in some of the recipes in this cookbook. Search out the brands with the least additives and the least sugar. Always choose full-fat versions. Buy the highest quality that you can find within your budget.

Xylitol

Xylitol is the natural sweetener that I use instead of sugar, because sugar makes you fatter faster than anything, and I'll hazard a guess that you don't want ice cream that makes you fatter. Xylitol has the same bulk and sweetness as sugar, but is a sugar alcohol which is not digested in the same way as other sugars are. Xylitol is safe for diabetics as it has a negligible glycemic load. A few people may experience slight intestinal discomfort when they start eating xylitol, but with regular consumption this goes away – don't ask me how I know.

The brand I use for the recipes in this book is Xyla, because it is made with 100% hardwoods (typically birch bark), and not corn. I do not recommend xylitol that is made with corn.

Xylitol is readily available online, but also available in stores. I buy it online and in bulk because it is a lot cheaper per pound that way. You could start a xylitol co-op!

In the sugar-free marshmallow recipe I specify powdered xylitol. I urge you to buy this ready powdered if you can, rather than make your own. Those lovely xylitol producers have something far more powerful than even a Vitamix for pulverizing stuff to a dust. Powdered xylitol is imperceptible on the tongue and dissolves in a heartbeat – you will not get that result from your home blender. If you really cannot find powdered xylitol, then blend the living daylights out of your granular xylitol to get it as fine as you can.

NOTE: You cannot use erythritol (or erythritol blends) in place of xylitol in these recipes! They are formulated for xylitol. Erythritol behaves very differently. If you ignore this, your ice cream will set like a block of ice. Don't say I didn't warn you.

Dog owners please note: like chocolate, xylitol is dangerous to dogs – do not let them share your xylitol-containing goodies!

Vanilla 100% Whey Protein Powder

In the first version of this cookbook I used whey protein powder (or egg white powder) to increase the protein content of the ice creams. Having moved the focus of this cookbook to a ketogenic – as opposed to low carb – diet, protein requirements have reduced. Also, when I originally wrote this cookbook in 2013, there was really only one great whey protein powder on the market – Optimum Nutrition Gold Standard 100% Whey Vanilla Protein Powder. Fast forward nearly 4 years and there are hundreds of whey protein powders available, which makes it **really** complicated and difficult for anyone wanting to use them in recipes, because they're all different – different ingredients, different flavors, different sweeteners, different...you get the picture. There are now **way** too many variables for me to guarantee everyone a great result when using whey protein powders. It has also become apparent that the formulation of the Optimum Nutrition whey has changed, so I can no longer recommend it.

Bottom line: the recipes in this book no longer require whey protein powder or egg white powder, but if you need to increase your protein intake you can add either of them to the ice creams. Bear in mind the whey protein powder will affect the taste of the finished ice cream, and you're on your own when it comes to choosing one as I can't possibly taste and test every whey powder available on the market today. Egg white powder will likely require a small increase in the amount of xylitol used in the recipe.

- Always add the whey protein or egg white powder at the end, right before the guar gum, and only blend just long enough to mix them in – so only for about 10 seconds. The best way to add it is to turn the blender to low and slowly pour the powder through the hole in the blender lid in a steady stream.

Guar gum

Since my ice creams do not use egg yolks to emulsify them, I use guar gum to help give a very smooth and creamy emulsion, and to improve the texture of the finished, frozen ice cream. Guar gum is made from ground guar beans and is an emulsifier and thickener. It also does magical things to ice crystals. We love that.

Do not be tempted to switch out guar gum with xanthan gum – they are not interchangeable when it comes to ice cream. I knew you'd want to ask me, so I thought I'd just put it straight out there.

When making your ice cream base, be careful to follow the instructions and add the guar gum last, and do not blend the ice cream base for longer than 30 seconds after you have added it. If you over mix the base after the guar gum is added you will get a very gluey, chewy ice cream.

Guar gum is readily available online and increasingly available in grocery stores. Guar gum is not cheap, but you only use tiny amounts, so it will last you a long, long time. Store guar gum in an air-tight jar. I used Bob's Red Mill brand guar gum in these recipes.

Sea salt

Salt is used to brighten the delicate flavors in ice cream and to stop them from tasting flat. I highly recommend using coarse sea salt instead of regular table salt, both for the improved flavor, and the higher concentration of minerals found in sea salt. Oh, and measure it. It takes 1 second longer. Salt is not a good ice cream flavor if your eye-balling goes a bit awry.

Additional Ingredients

Alcohol

Alcohol has two uses in ice cream – it adds flavor and inhibits freezing. A splash of liquor can transform the flavor of an ice cream from ordinary to fantastic, and most usually with just a very small amount. It can also be used in small amounts to alter the texture and consistency of the finished frozen ice cream. Altering the freeze-ability of ice cream does not require much alcohol, while adding a lot will prevent your ice cream from freezing at all. This is why people typically do not feel cold when they've been on the jolly juice. They either can't feel it, or they don't care.

I buy miniature bottles both to minimize the cost and so I don't have loads of spirits lying around the joint looking for trouble. I don't want the cats getting into it.

Butter

There's not a lot of butter involved in these recipes, but when there is some called for, I highly recommend using butter from grass-fed cows, produced without the use of hormones or antibiotics. I use Kerrygold Irish Butter in my recipes. It's awesome and it reminds me of my homeland. I'm British, it's close enough.

Cocoa Powder, 100% Chocolate, and Cocoa Nibs

My preferred brand for all things chocolate is Valrhona, which is made in France. It's kinda pricey and is not always readily available everywhere…but the flavor and the smoothness? Oooh la la! If you can get it, I thoroughly recommend using it.

Valrhona's Head Chocolatier is Frederic Bau, and he can do things with chocolate that would make you gasp out loud and your knees wobble. Frederic kissed me once. I didn't wash for a week. I should clarify that this incident has nothing to do with my belief that Valrhona is the best chocolate on earth. The French kiss everything.

If you can't find Valrhona, buy the best cocoa products that you have available. Other good brands in the US are Ghirardelli and Scharffenberger.

Cocoa powder / cacao / raw cocoa must be unsweetened – always read the label to verify. There should be nothing but cocoa in it. Some manufacturers can be pretty darn sneaky these days. One of my life mottos is "Read the label!" Words to live by, right there.

100% chocolate (which has no sugar in it) can be harder to find, but Ghirardelli and Scharffenberger both make it in retail packs. Any chocolate which has a lower percentage of cocoa in it than 100%, has sugar in it – and the lower the % of cocoa, the higher the % of sugar. Most people cannot eat 100% chocolate on its own as it is very bitter; it needs recipes developed specifically for it to be edible. The very good news is that your 100% chocolate stash won't go missing from the pantry when you're not looking. Well, it might once, but never a second time.

Cocoa nibs are whole cocoa beans that have been roasted and then crushed into little pieces. They are 100% cocoa. They are slightly bitter-tasting, but can add a deep chocolate flavor and great crunch when used well in recipes. I use them instead of chocolate chips, since chocolate chips have sugar in them and we don't want any of that sugar shenanigans going on.

I used Valrhona 100% Cocoa Powder, Ghirardelli 100% Cacao Unsweetened Chocolate, and Valrhona Cocoa Nibs in these recipes.

Extracts / essences

Extracts and essences are concentrated natural flavors – the base used is typically either alcohol or oil – that allow the addition of a whole lot of flavor without adding a whole ton of stuff. Think adding half a teaspoon of orange extract instead of 2 whole oranges. Extracts and essences can intensify the flavor of the ice cream without changing the ratio of fat, water and sugar in the custard.

Always use pure extracts and essences with no added sugar, and be sure that you are buying extracts, essences, and natural flavorings. Avoid anything that has "imitation" or "artificial" on the label. We only want the real deal in our ice creams. Oh, and in our bodies.

Fruits

These recipes focus on using only the most nutrient dense fruits, and those with the lowest amounts of sugar – mainly berries and (some) citrus. Choose the best quality and freshest fruits available. For the most nutrition, use fruits when they are naturally in season, although frozen berries are very useful as they are typically cheaper than fresh, and can mean affordable fabulous fruit ice creams in the middle of winter. When buying frozen berries make sure they are unsweetened. I like to buy fresh berries in bulk (or pay a visit to a local pick-your-own farm) when they are in season, and freeze them so I have a supply all year.

Glycerin

Glycerin is extremely useful in small amounts to stop things from freezing too hard, and to improve texture. Like xylitol, glycerin is a sugar alcohol that has a negligible glycemic load, being digested differently to regular sugars. Glycerin is 60% as sweet as regular sugar, and derived from fats, typically coconut if it is vegetable glycerin. Glycerin performs wizardry in recipes where it is included. Yes, I know you are a little wary of strange ingredients you haven't used before, but you cannot swap out or leave out the glycerin from a recipe and still get a successful result. The recipes that use it rely on it to do their thing. Get yourself some glycerin. It also makes a fantastic skin moisturizer. Would I lie to you about baby soft skin?

I use vegetable glycerin in my recipes – make sure it is food grade – which is readily available online if you cannot find it in local stores. In stores it's best to just ask because sometimes it is with the skin care, sometimes it is with the supplements, sometimes with the first aid, and sometimes in the pharmacy. This stuff gets around a bit. I use Now brand.

Konjac Flour (Glucomannan Powder)

I use konjac flour – also known as glucomannan powder – to replace cornstarch or flour as a thickener. It is a soluble plant fiber that thickens with 10x the power of cornstarch, so a little goes a very long way. It is tasteless, easy to use, and can be used in all sorts of cooking applications for thickening and gelling. It is readily available online or in stores that sell supplements. No, there is no other KETO thickener that comes even vaguely close to the awesomeness that konjac flour does. TRUST ME. Just get some. You'll thank me. Repeatedly.

Nuts

Nuts are a great way to add crunch and flavor to ice creams. Always use fresh nuts as they contain oils which will go rancid over time, and especially in warm conditions. It is best to store nuts in the freezer to keep them as fresh as possible.

Many recipes call for the nuts to be toasted. The easiest way to do this is to spread them on a cookie sheet and pop them under the broiler (grill), turning them regularly. Nuts can burn very quickly, so don't walk away once the nuts are under the heat. No one likes burnt nuts.

When buying coconut, always make sure it is unsweetened; check the label to be sure – there is a lot of sneaky sugar-adding going on in many brands. You need to be your very own Food Police.

Spices

Spices are awesome. They can perk up the most ordinary of dishes into something rather swoon-worthy. Cardamom is my favorite spice ever. I first ate it in San Francisco, and I have loved that city ever since.

I prefer to buy my spices in small amounts, as I need them, from a store that sells them loose, rather than buying pre-packaged jars that I may not use up before they go stale and lose their potency. Spices sold in jars are also significantly more expensive than buying loose. Store spices in air-tight glass containers, and keep them in a cool, dark place.

EQUIPMENT

In the equipment department, the only thing you MUST have is a churner, so don't panic thinking that you're going to have to mortgage the house to make these healthy ice creams – you're not. Everything else listed here just makes it easier, and quicker, but since I know you'll ask me what stuff I use, I thought I'd just give you the list upfront.

A handy link to all the equipment I use can be found on page 27

Ice Cream Churner

There are lots to choose from, ranging from super-duper, super-expensive commercial models, to buckets with rock salt round them. I am only going to tell you about the ones I have because between them they have successfully churned thousands of gallons of ice cream perfectly. And I don't mean any old ice cream – I mean "that was the best ice cream I've eaten in my life" ice cream.

Don't think for one second that you must go all big and fancy in the churner department – you don't. This one is all you need – a Cuisinart ICE-21 Automatic 1 ½ Quart Ice Cream Maker. I do also have a Cuisinart ICE- 100 Compressor Ice Cream Maker, but you definitely don't need to spring for this type of machine to get fantastic ice cream.

Having used both I can confidently say that neither makes better ice cream than the other. The only advantage to the compressor type of churner is that you can churn ice cream 24 hours a day if you want to, as opposed to waiting for the freezer bowls to re-freeze before you can use them again. If you have the money, don't have the space in your freezer for bowls, or see yourself churning ice cream in large quantities or want a host of different flavors all ready at once then go ahead and get a compressor type. Otherwise, the much cheaper freezer bowl model will give you ice cream that is every bit as good.

Check out our podcast on churners: http://www.ketovangelistkitchen.com/episode-40-ice-cream-churners/ for the full scoop (sorry, I couldn't help myself).

If you want to look at other brands I recommend that you read as many consumer reviews as you can before making your decision.

Weighing Scale

If you follow my blogs I can just imagine your eyes rolling right around your sockets about now, because you've heard me beat this drum SO. MANY. TIMES. Oh, and here she goes again.

There is only one way to get accurate, consistent, fantastic results every single time you make great ice cream, and that is to weigh your non-liquid ingredients. Cups are handy, and super useful for liquids, but they are just not accurate enough for consistent results when ratios of ingredients matter. I weigh everything. Every time.

The scale I use has a flat weighing plate, a pull-out digital display, and weighs in both metric and imperial. It also has the ability to zero out what is on the display so you can weigh directly into the container, bowl or blender jug of your choice, which means less work and less dirty dishes. We love that.

If you don't have a kitchen scale, please avail yourself of one. Trade in your bathroom scale for one, put one on your Christmas list, bat your eyes at your spouse, or barter your homegrown lettuces in exchange for one. Just get one. Please. Thank you.

High Powered Blender OR Blender OR Food processor

A Vitamix or Blendtec will be your very best friend for ice cream. Smooth, smooth, smooth. These machines smash everything that goes in them into liquid – except raspberry seeds – and believe me, I have tried to pulverize those suckers on numerous occasions. Notwithstanding the raspberry seed issue, high powered blenders are amazing. I even take mine on vacation with me, and I would not joke about such things.

I also have a second jug for my Vitamix – I find having a second blending container incredibly handy. Or maybe I just don't like washing up when I am on a roll in the kitchen. Either way, second blending jug = goodness.

I have a Kitchen Aid 5-speed blender in addition to my Vitamix for those times when I don't want to pulverize everything into oblivion. Some things don't require the extra power. I use my regular blender when I don't want or need to use the Vitamix. Grinding nuts is a great example – try grinding nuts in a Vitamix and you'll have awesome nut butter, but you won't have any ground nuts.

I also have a Cuisinart Elite 14-cup Food Processor. It comes with three bowls that sit inside one another so you can do three different things before you have to wash up, and I love that. It also has a large capacity, which I find very useful when making large batches of ice cream. Or anything else, come to think of it. I find some ice cream recipes easier to get out of a food processor than a Vitamix. Your call.

If you have one of the three you'll be good for making great ice cream.

Spatulas

You can never have too many flexible spatulas lying around when you're in the middle of ice cream production. You specifically need spatulas that will not damage the inside of your ice cream machine's bowl while you're removing the ice cream. Rubber is good, as is silicone. Smooth and super flexible is the kind of spatulas we are after.

I use the plastic spatulas that came with my ice cream churners ONLY for removing ice cream from the machine, because they are perfect for this task and I want them in tip-top condition.

Sieves

I am a perfectionist, so I use sieves a lot. A lot. Strawberry seeds in the sauce? Sieve. Hazelnut skins? Sieve. Cocoa powder? Sieve. Nut dust in the nuts you just chopped? Sieve. Ice cream custards? Sieve. I sieve everything in the name of texture perfection. And when it comes to ice cream – in my little world – texture perfection is mandatory. Sieving is important.

I'll forgive you for not having sieve-itis with most things, but not when it comes to ice cream. You need a sieve (or two). And you need those sieves to be really good fine mesh sieves. These are not your regular flour-sifting sieves. When I say fine, I mean *really* fine. The kind of fine that will stop strawberry seeds in their tracks. With traditional egg-based ice creams I sieve every single custard. You won't need to do that with all my ice cream recipes, but some of them you will, so where it says in the recipe instructions to sieve, please do. I have 3 fine mesh sieves in different sizes. Please buy at least one really good fine mesh sieve. Thank you.

Glass Storage

I am not a fan of plastic for storage. At all. For anything. And especially my ice cream custards.

Once my custards are made, I pour them from the blender directly into wide-mouth Mason (with screw –on lid) or Le Parfait (with bail and gasket lid) jars. Le Parfait are expensive in the US but I love the ones I bought in England a hundred years ago that have since travelled around the world with me. Either of these jars make storing and chilling ice cream custards super easy. They take up minimal space in the fridge, they stack, and you can stir and pour the custards directly into your churner when you're ready. There's no need to empty the custard into a bowl to stir before churning, just stick your spatula into the jar. Boom!

This saves time, and more importantly, a lot of wasted ice cream custard because you are not transferring from one container to another. Plus, they make pouring your custard into your churner super-easy and super-clean; which means less clean up. I know you want less clean up.

Once the custards are churned I use lidded glass Pyrex dishes for storing my ice cream in the freezer. If plastic is capable of absorbing colors and flavors, it follows that the plastic is not impermeable. The thought that the chemicals in plastic are merrily transferring back into my ice cream is highly unpleasant to me. In the Brown house, it's got to be glass. Specifically, I use the Pyrex 7-cup round dishes for ice cream storage, but the rectangular 6-cup ones work well, too.

Dipping Forks

These are cheap and nice to have, but not essential, for dipping the macadamia nuts in the Ballistic Coffee recipe. They make life a lot easier (and prettier), but since the dipped nuts are going into ice cream, pretty is not super-important. If you don't have a dipping fork, you can use a regular fork instead.

Other Equipment

I also have on hand:

- Glass mixing bowls
- Electric hand mixer
- Knives
- Measuring cups (for liquids)
- Measuring spoons (for spices, extracts, guar gum, etc.)
- Microplanes (for zesting)
- Whisks – small, medium, large

MIXING, CHURNING, AND FREEZING

Mixing, churning and freezing play critical roles in the production of great ice cream. How you mix, churn and freeze your ice cream custard can make a significant difference to the final result. The difference between ice cream and gelato, for example, is nothing to do with ingredients or ratios, and everything to do with how it is churned. Mixing, churning, and freezing are really important, so I implore you to pay attention. And I don't implore very often.

Before we start mixing and churning the ice cream custard, you should be aware that the flavors only fully develop once they are completely frozen. The finished frozen ice cream will taste different from both the liquid custard, and from the freshly churned ice cream in your churner, so bear that in mind when you're licking that spatula! I recommend keeping your spoons on hold until the ice cream is completely frozen in the freezer. You cannot judge an ice cream by its custard.

Ice cream making is actually pretty complicated, scientifically speaking. There's a whole bunch of geekery around getting ice crystals to form the right way, not getting them to freeze too hard, or too soft, and other thrilling physics dilemmas to think about – and there are tons of little tips and tricks that will help you get that perfect scoop of deliciousness every time.

Even if you are not new to the world of homemade ice cream, you are new to these healthy ice creams, and these custards do not behave like traditional ice cream custards. Yes, I am about to implore, again. After waiting this long for fabulously healthy ice cream recipes – and getting this far in the book – I don't want you to be disappointed with your results.

I highly recommend making a few of the simpler recipes first so you get a feel for how these ice cream custards behave, and so you know what to expect. Then, when you make the more complex ones you'll be a Pro.

Mixing

We need to get serious for a minute, and talk about air. Because air is really important in Ice Cream Land. The incorporation of air into ice cream custards during mixing will materially change the outcome of your final frozen ice cream, and it all depends on how you mix and for how long you mix.

Traditional ice creams made with an egg custard have very little air incorporated into them in the mixing stage. This produces that dense, creamy texture that we all love about premium ice cream. Cheaper ice creams have a lot of air pumped into them during mixing, which produces a much lighter, fluffier ice cream. Light and fluffy is great for the manufacturers since they are essentially selling a lot of air and a little bit of ice cream. This is one of the reasons that premium ice creams are more expensive – you literally get more ice cream – even though the container may be the same size as the cheaper versions. If you have ever let cheap ice cream melt completely, you'll notice there ain't a lot of ice cream in the bottom of your bowl, because all the air has gone away.

With these super-healthy recipes, the goal is to get as close to that dense, creamy texture of traditional ice creams as we can, so we want to incorporate as little air as possible during mixing. Traditional ice creams have you stirring slowly in a pan to make the custard base. These recipes use a blender, and blenders add air.

Then along comes our friend, guar gum. Guar gum makes the ice cream custard into an emulsion – which is a very wonderful thing – but once an emulsion is formed, air gets trapped faster and more easily than ever. We don't want that.

So now you know what the goal is, and why, here are your mixing tips and tricks:

- Blend for as short a time as possible just to mix the ingredients together. When the recipe says 10 seconds, it means no more than 10 seconds. Counting is your friend.
- Blend on as low a speed as possible to get the job done. Higher speed = more air whipped in.
- Always add the guar gum last. Tap the gum into the mixture through the opening in the lid while the blender is running and then turn it off.
- Do not over blend, especially once you have added the guar gum. 30 seconds on the lowest speed to ensure it is completely distributed and then you're done.
- Leave the ice cream custard to rest overnight in the 'fridge. Not only does this allow the custard to get super-cold (very important for churning) but it also allows air to escape from the custard. Perhaps most importantly though, this resting allows the magic to happen between the ingredients - the proteins, fats, "sugars", water and emulsifiers bond together and create a much better texture ice cream. Ice cream is science – just give it some time.
- Just before pouring the custard into the churner, stir the custard with a spatula really well – to help eliminate more trapped air bubbles and make sure it is thoroughly mixed. Some custards firm up during the chilling stage and this will re-liquefy them so you can pour them into the churner.

Churning and Freezing

As with mixing, churning adds air. Churning incorporates less air, less quickly than mixing because it churns at a much slower speed, and the churner has wide paddles rather than skinny blades like a blender.

Churning encourages the ice cream custard to form small ice crystals instead of large ones as it freezes. Churning also enables the ice cream to freeze uniformly. The faster your ice cream freezes in the churner, the better texture your final frozen ice cream will be.

The goal is to churn your ice cream custard in as short a time as possible, so you incorporate the least amount of air, and so that the ice cream does not have time to make large ice crystals. Give ice crystals an inch and they take a mile.

Your biggest aid in this churning endeavor is having everything super cold before you begin.

Here are your churning and freezing tips and tricks:

- If you live in a hot climate – or if it's just a hot day where you are – churn in the coolest part of the day, and in the coolest room in the house. Have the A/C on. Have the fans on. Think cool.
- If you are using a churner with a removable freezer bowl that needs to be pre-frozen, make sure that it is completely frozen before you churn. If you shake it and there is ANY noise, it is not ready to use. Overnight is typically sufficient to freeze the bowl but it may need up to 24 hours depending on how cold your freezer is. Plan well.
- Your ice cream custard needs to be *really* cold before you churn it. To be really cold it needs to be refrigerated for at least 8 hours, and preferably overnight. DO NOT TRY AND CHURN THE ICE CREAM CUSTARD IF IT IS NOT COLD. All that will happen is that it will churn for so long that the freezer bowl starts to defrost and then all you are doing is incorporating air into custard that is not getting frozen. You will be sad.
- All your equipment should be as cold as possible before you start churning: the dasher (stirring paddle), any jug that you use to pour the custard into the churner, and the spatulas. I even chill the paddle in the freezer.
- Do not get the freezer bowl out of the freezer until you are ready to use it straight away.
- Do not assume that the custard you make from one of these recipes will all fit in your churner in one batch. There are too many variables for me to be able to produce recipes that are exactly the right quantity for every churner available. Be prepared to churn in two batches at times. Unless you allow your freezer bowl to defrost completely, you will be able to churn the second batch very quickly after the first. Just make sure that you rinse (in cold water) the freezer bowl, and get it back in the freezer as fast as possible once you have removed the first batch of churned ice cream.
- Do not overfill the churning bowl with ice cream custard. Ice cream increases in volume as it churns since air is being incorporated. If you overfill the churner the ice cream will take too long to freeze, will churn for too long, and you'll have a big mess as it starts coming out of the top of the churner. None of these are desirable outcomes. Doing two smaller batches is much better than trying to churn too big a batch.
- These ice cream recipes typically take longer to churn than traditional ice creams, and they are also softer when churned. If you have churned traditional ice cream this may throw you until you get used to it. These ice creams do not churn to more than soft-serve consistency. They finish freezing in the deep freeze.
- Place the empty container that you are going to put the churned ice cream into, in the freezer when you start churning so it is super-cold when the ice cream has churned.
- Once you have put the churned ice cream in the cold storage container, cover the surface with wax or parchment paper, put the lid on, and place it in the deep freezer immediately.

- If you have a separate "deep" freeze, put your freshly churned ice cream in that freezer initially, so it freezes as fast and firm as possible. The next day you can transfer it to the freezer part of your kitchen 'fridge/freezer.
- Once churned, freeze the ice cream in the deep freezer for at least 8 hours before serving, and preferably overnight. Really, try and wait, or churn just before bedtime so you're not tempted to dig in straight away.

Once your ice cream has completely frozen, it is ready to scoop and eat – finally! Your patience is about to be rewarded. BIG TIME.

Here's a few final points to note about these ice creams that is different to traditional ice creams:

- The use of guar gum as an emulsifier creates an ice cream that is less dense than traditional home-made ice cream, so they have a tendency to melt faster once they are out of the deep freeze. Bear this is in mind when you are getting ready to serve your ice cream. They do not need to be taken out of the freezer ahead of time like many premium ice creams do.
- Do not keep your ice cream out of the freezer any longer than is necessary. Once you have scooped, get the ice cream container back in the freezer as fast as you can.
- They do not travel as well as traditional ice creams because they melt faster.
- Once melted, they won't re-freeze as well, so it is best to re-churn it (if it is an ice cream that does not have mix-ins added).

Now, let's get in the kitchen and get our ice cream on!

COOKING RESOURCES AND Q & A

This cookbook isn't an introduction to a ketogenic or low-carb way of life. It's a how-to-make-fantastic-ice-cream guide, and a collection of ketogenic recipes that will blow your taste buds and your mind.

I have included chapters on ingredients and equipment specific to this cookbook, which give you an overview of some of the things that might be unfamiliar to you.

However, many of you are new to this way of eating and all that involves. You might also be new to cooking if you've always relied on regular ice cream from the store, or even regular ice cream made at home. So, there might be a few new-to-you ingredients or pieces of equipment that are not detailed in the preceding chapters. I'm including links to the information on my website, so if you need it you can easily grab it, and if you don't need it then you won't have to rifle through that info to get to the recipes.

If you do find you still have questions about ingredients, equipment, or recipes – after checking out the online info at the links included here – there's a Q&A page for this cookbook on my website. Head there and see if the answer is already waiting for you. Feel free to add new questions in the comments and I will update the page with answers as they come in.

Now, let's get cooking!

INFORMATION ON INGREDIENTS

www.carriebrown.com/archives/23109

INFORMATION ON EQUIPMENT

www.carriebrown.com/archives/23310

THE KETO ICE CREAM SCOOP Q&A

www.carriebrown.com/keto-ice-cream-scoop-cookbook-qa

You Had Me At Hazelnut Ice Cream

1 cup / 8 fl oz. hemp milk, unsweetened (see page 12)

1 ½ cups / 12 fl oz. heavy cream (see page 12)

2 TBSP vegetable glycerin

3 ½ oz. / 100g xylitol (NO substitutes!)

½ tsp. sea salt

7 oz. / 195g roasted hazelnuts, skins removed

1 tsp. vanilla extract

2 oz. / 55g cream cheese (full fat)

½ tsp. guar gum

½ batch Chocolate Chunks - (recipe page 93) – this needs to be made and frozen in advance

Warm the hemp milk, cream, glycerin, xylitol, and sea salt in a medium pan until it just starts to boil. Remove from the heat, add the roasted hazelnuts, cover and leave for 2 hours to soak. Soaking your nuts is important!

Carefully pour the soaked hazelnuts and cream in a blender and blend for 4 – 5 minutes until the nuts are completely smooth. I mean COMPLETELY SMOOTH. Test it. They gotta be smooth.

Add the cream cheese and vanilla extract and blend until the cheese is completely mixed in. It will be super thick. While the blender is still running, add the guar gum by tapping it through the opening in the lid, and blend for 30 seconds.

Pour the ice cream custard into a bowl or jar, cover, and place in the 'fridge for at least 8 hours, but preferably overnight. Don't skip the chillin', no matter which type of churner you have.

Stir the chilled custard well – THIS ONE WILL TAKE A LOT OF STIRRING! – to make sure it is completely mixed and read the churning and freezing section on page 23. Freeze the custard in your churner according to the manufacturer's instructions. It typically takes between 15 - 20 minutes to freeze to a soft-serve consistency.

Once the ice cream has frozen to a soft-serve consistency, quickly transfer it from the churning bowl into your pre-chilled container and quickly stir in the Chocolate Chunks evenly through the custard.

Place in the freezer for at least 8 hours, preferably overnight.

~~~~~~

"This is the best thing I have ever eaten in my life" **–** Brian Williamson

Va-va-voom Vanilla Ice Cream

1 ½ cups / 12 fl oz. almond milk, unsweetened vanilla

1 whole vanilla pod, split lengthwise, seeds scraped out

3 ½ oz. / 100g xylitol (NO substitutes!)

1 tsp. sea salt

1 cup / 8 fl oz. heavy cream (see page 12)

1 ½ cups / 12 fl oz. thick coconut milk (see page 11)

1 tsp. vanilla extract

1 tsp. guar gum

Warm the almond milk, vanilla seeds and pod, xylitol, sea salt, and cream in a medium pan until it just starts to boil. Simmer for one minute and then remove from the heat, cover, and leave for an hour to steep.

Pour the vanilla-infused milk through a sieve to remove the vanilla pod.

Place the thick coconut milk in a blender with the vanilla-infused milk, and the vanilla extract, and blend for 10 seconds.

Turn the blender to low speed, and while the blender is running, add the guar gum by tapping it through the opening in the lid, and blend for 30 seconds.

Pour the ice cream custard into a bowl or jar, cover, and place in the 'fridge for at least 8 hours, but preferably overnight. Don't skip the chillin', no matter which type of churner you have.

Stir the chilled custard well to make sure it is completely mixed, and read the churning and freezing section on page 23. Freeze the custard in your churner according to the manufacturer's instructions. It typically takes between 15 – 25 minutes to freeze to a soft-serve consistency.

Once the ice cream has frozen to a soft-serve consistency, quickly transfer it from the churning bowl into your pre-chilled container, and place in the freezer for at least 8 hours, preferably overnight.

~~~~~~

If I'm honest, vanilla ice cream never really floated my boat growing up. The use of real, live vanilla pods crammed full of tiny, heavily-scented specks of deliciousness sure changed my mind on the whole darn vanilla-is-dull thing. Will you just look at all those adorable little black speckles? I still won't choose a dish of vanilla on its own, but it is a heaven-sent addition to any number of other desserts, or simple bowl of ripe, fresh berries. Yay, vanilla pods!

Caffeination Station Ice Cream

1 ¼ cup / 10 fl oz. almond milk, unsweetened vanilla

5 oz. / 140g whole coffee beans

5 oz. / 140g xylitol (NO substitutes!)

1 tsp. sea salt

¾ cup / 6 fl oz. heavy cream (see page 12)

1 ½ cups / 12 fl oz. thick coconut milk (see page 11)

1 TBSP whole coffee beans, finely ground

1 tsp. vanilla extract

1 tsp. guar gum

In a pan, bring the almond milk, whole coffee beans, xylitol, sea salt, and cream to the boil over a medium heat. Stir. Remove from the heat, cover and leave to steep for an hour.

Strain the coffee-infused mixture through a sieve to remove the beans.

Place the thick coconut milk into a blender, and add the coffee-infused milk, the ground coffee, and the vanilla extract, and blend for 10 seconds.

Turn the blender to low speed, and while the blender is running, add the guar gum by tapping it through the opening in the lid, and blend for 30 seconds.

Pour the ice cream custard into a bowl or jar, cover, and place in the 'fridge for at least 8 hours, but preferably overnight. Don't skip the chillin', no matter which type of churner you have.

Stir the chilled custard well to make sure it is completely mixed and read the churning and freezing section on page 23. Freeze the custard in your churner according to the manufacturer's instructions. It typically takes between 15 - 20 minutes to freeze to a soft-serve consistency.

Once the ice cream has frozen to a soft-serve consistency, quickly transfer it from the churning bowl into your pre-chilled container, and place in the freezer for at least 8 hours, preferably overnight.

Note: because of the extra sweetener required for this flavor, the ice cream does not freeze as hard as most. If you can store it in a deep freezer instead of your 'fridge / freezer, I would recommend that you do so. Be very fast when taking it out of the freezer to serve.

~~~~~~

Your kitchen will smell like a coffee roasters by the time you're done steeping. I found this to be an entirely fantastic side benefit. Just saying. Also use the old beans to fertilize your roses.

Butter Me Up Pecan Ice Cream

1 oz. / 30g butter

5 ¼ oz. / 150g pecan halves

¼ tsp. sea salt

1 ½ cups / 12 fl oz. almond milk, unsweetened vanilla

1 cup / 8 fl oz. heavy cream (see page 12)

3 ½ oz. / 100g xylitol (NO substitutes!)

1 tsp. sea salt

1 tsp. vanilla extract

1 cup / 8 fl oz. thick coconut milk (see page 11)

2 oz. / 55g butter, softened

1 tsp. guar gum

Preheat the oven to 350F. Melt the butter in a small pan. Remove from the heat, add the pecans and salt, and stir until the nuts are well coated with butter.

Spread evenly on a baking sheet and toast in the oven for 10 minutes, stirring occasionally, until golden brown. Remove from the oven. Try not to eat them all.

Once the nuts are completely cooled, chop them roughly and store in an airtight container in the freezer.

Place the almond milk, cream, xylitol, sea salt, vanilla extract, thick coconut milk, and butter in a blender and blend for 10 seconds.

Turn the blender to low speed, and while the blender is running, add the guar gum by tapping it through the opening in the lid, and blend for 30 seconds.

Pour the ice cream custard into a bowl or jar, cover, and place in the 'fridge for at least 8 hours, but preferably overnight. Don't skip the chillin', no matter which type of churner you have.

Stir the chilled custard well to make sure it is completely mixed and read the churning and freezing section on page 23. Freeze the custard in your churner according to the manufacturer's instructions. It typically takes between 15 - 20 minutes to freeze to a soft-serve consistency.

Once the ice cream has frozen to a soft-serve consistency in the churner, add the chopped frozen buttered pecan pieces and churn until mixed through.

Quickly transfer the ice cream from the churning bowl into your pre-chilled container, cover and place in the freezer for at least 8 hours, preferably overnight.

Kept In The Dark Chocolate Ice Cream

1 ½ cups / 12 fl oz. hemp milk, unsweetened (see page 12)

½ cup / 4 fl oz. heavy cream (see page 12)

5 ¼ oz. / 150g xylitol (NO substitutes!)

½ tsp. sea salt

1 ¼ oz. / 35g raw, unsweetened cocoa powder

2 oz. / 55g 100% cocoa solids chocolate (unsweetened), chopped

1 ½ cups / 12 fl oz. thick coconut milk (see page 11)

1 tsp. vanilla extract

½ tsp. guar gum

Place the hemp milk, cream, xylitol, sea salt, and cocoa powder in a pan over medium heat and whisk until the cocoa powder is completely mixed in. Bring to the boil, reduce the heat, and simmer for 1 minute, whisking constantly.

Remove pan from the heat and stir in the chopped chocolate.

Leave to cool, stirring well occasionally.

Place the thick coconut milk and vanilla extract in the blender, add the cooled chocolate custard and blend for 10 seconds.

Turn the blender to low speed, and while the blender is running, add the guar gum by tapping it through the opening in the lid, and blend for 30 seconds.

Pour the ice cream custard into a bowl or jar, cover, and place in the 'fridge for at least 8 hours, but preferably overnight. Don't skip the chillin', no matter which type of churner you have.

Stir the chilled custard well to make sure it is completely mixed and read the churning and freezing section on page 23. Freeze the custard in your churner according to the manufacturer's instructions. It typically takes between 15 - 20 minutes to freeze to a soft-serve consistency.

Once the ice cream has frozen to a soft-serve consistency, quickly transfer it from the churning bowl into your pre-chilled container, and place in the freezer for at least 8 hours, preferably overnight.

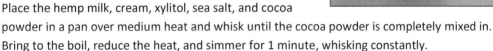

Chocolate Ice Cream how it ought to be: deep, dark, and decidedly delicious. And good for you.

Pistachio Rose Ice Cream

1 ¼ cups / 10 fl oz. heavy cream (see page 12)

3 ½ oz. / 100g xylitol (NO substitutes!)

½ tsp. sea salt

4 TBSP rose water

1 tsp. rose extract

1 cup / 8 fl oz. thin coconut milk (see page 11)

7 ½ oz. / 210g crème fraiche

1 tsp. guar gum

3 oz. / 85g pistachio pieces, toasted and frozen

Warm the cream, xylitol, sea salt, rose water, and rose extract in a medium pan until it just starts to boil. Simmer for 1 minute and then remove from the heat and cool for 15 minutes.

Carefully pour the warm cream mixture into a blender, add the thin coconut milk and crème fraiche and blend for 10 seconds.

Turn the blender to low speed, and while the blender is running, add the guar gum by tapping it through the opening in the lid, and blend for 30 seconds.

Pour the ice cream custard into a bowl or jar, cover, and place in the 'fridge for at least 8 hours, but preferably overnight. Don't skip the chillin', no matter which type of churner you have.

Stir the chilled custard well to make sure it is completely mixed and read the churning and freezing section on page 23. Freeze the custard in your churner according to the manufacturer's instructions. It typically takes between 15 - 20 minutes to freeze to a soft-serve consistency.

Once the ice cream has frozen to a soft-serve consistency in the churner, pour the frozen pistachio pieces through the opening in the top of the churner and churn until mixed through.

Quickly transfer it from the churning bowl into your pre-chilled container and place in the freezer for at least 8 hours, preferably overnight.

~~~~~~

One of my very favorite things growing up was Rose Turkish Delight. We only had it once a year, so it was one of the absolute highlights of my childhood Christmases. I could easily have eaten a whole box in one go had I been allowed. My sweet tooth knew no bounds. Now Turkish Delight and its zillion sugary carbs are off the menu, I am completely crushing that craving with this sublime rose ice cream studded with toasted pistachios. Also, the scent of roses is like crack to me, so this incredibly smooth and creamy concoction is simply swoon-worthy.

Butterscotch Bling Ice Cream

1 ½ cups / 12 fl oz. almond milk, unsweetened vanilla

3 oz. / 85g xylitol (NO substitutes!)

½ tsp. sea salt

1 ½ TBSP butterscotch extract

1 ½ TBSP bourbon

1 cup / 8 fl oz. heavy cream (see page 12)

1 oz. / 30g butter

½ cup / 4 fl oz. thick coconut milk (see page 11)

4 oz. / 110g cream cheese (full fat)

2 tsp. cocoa powder, sieved

½ tsp. guar gum

4 oz. / 110g slivered almonds, toasted, and frozen

½ batch Chocolate Fudge Ripple (recipe page 87) – this needs to be made in advance

Warm the almond milk, xylitol, sea salt, butterscotch extract, bourbon, and cream in a medium pan until it just starts to boil. Remove from the heat, add the butter and stir until the butter is melted.

Place the thick coconut milk, cream cheese, and cocoa powder in a blender with the warm butterscotch cream, and blend on low until completely smooth.

With the blender still on low speed, and while the blender is running, add the guar gum by tapping it through the opening in the lid, and blend for 30 seconds.

Pour the ice cream custard into a bowl or jar, cover, and place in the 'fridge for at least 8 hours, but preferably overnight. Don't skip the chillin', no matter which type of churner you have.

Stir the chilled custard well to make sure it is completely mixed and read the churning and freezing section on page 23. Freeze the custard in your churner according to the manufacturer's instructions. It typically takes between 15 - 20 minutes to freeze to a soft-serve consistency.

Once the ice cream has frozen to a soft-serve consistency in the churner, add the toasted frozen almonds to the churner through the opening in the top, and churn until mixed through.

Quickly spoon a layer of ice cream into the bottom of your cold storage container. Spoon large dollops of Chocolate Fudge Ripple over the ice cream, and then continue to layer ice cream and fudge until the ice cream has all been removed from the churner. Be careful to 'dollop' the ice cream layer over the Fudge Ripple so that there is as little movement of the fudge as possible. Otherwise you will get 'muddy' ice cream. Cover and place in the freezer for at least 8 hours.

Immortal Avocado Ice Cream

1 cup / 8 fl oz. almond milk, unsweetened vanilla

½ cup / 4 fl oz. heavy cream (see page 12)

4 oz. / 110g sour cream

3 ½ oz. / 100g xylitol (NO substitutes!)

½ tsp. sea salt

1 TBSP white wine vinegar

2 TBSP vegetable glycerin

12 oz. / 335g avocado flesh (approx. 3 medium)

1 tsp. guar gum

Place the almond milk, cream, sour cream, xylitol, sea salt, white wine vinegar, and vegetable glycerin in a blender and blend for 10 seconds.

With the blender running on low, add the avocado flesh and guar gum through the hole in the blender lid and blend until smooth. It will be very thick and you might have to stop the blender and scrape down the sides a time or two.

This custard needs to be churned immediately! So, once the avocado cream is completely blended, read the churning and freezing section on page 23 and immediately freeze the custard in your churner according to the manufacturer's instructions. It typically takes between 10 - 15 minutes to freeze to a soft-serve consistency.

Once the ice cream has frozen to a soft-serve consistency, quickly transfer it from the churning bowl into your pre-chilled container, and place in the freezer for at least 8 hours, preferably overnight.

~~~~~~

What seems like the easiest recipe in the book was actually one of the ones that gave me the most grief. But, I persevered because I really wanted you (and me, if I'm honest) to have Avocado Ice Cream. Now you have a new way to enjoy the heck out of KETO's favorite fruit. And now you can use up all the over-ripe avocados you don't know what to do with but don't want to waste.

~~~~~~

Make an Avocado Milkshake for a fantastic summer drink!

Put 2 scoops of Immortal Avocado Ice Cream in a blender with ½ cup / 4 fl oz. almond milk, 2 ice cubes, and 2 tsps. xylitol and blend until smooth.

Toasted Triple Coconut Ice Cream

4 oz. / 110g flaked coconut, unsweetened

1 ½ cups / 12 fl oz. thick coconut milk (see page 11)

1 ¼ cup / 10 fl oz. thin coconut milk (see page 11)

3 ½ oz. / 100g xylitol (NO substitutes!)

¾ cup / 10 fl oz. heavy cream (see page 12)

1 tsp. sea salt

½ tsp. rum

1 tsp. guar gum

Spread the coconut on a baking sheet and toast under a broiler (grill) until lightly browned. Browning happens very quickly – do not walk away! Remove from under the broiler (grill) and leave to cool. Store in the freezer.

Place half (2 oz. / 55g) of the toasted coconut, the thick and thin coconut milks, xylitol, cream, sea salt, and rum in a pan and warm over medium heat until it just comes to the boil. Remove from the heat and leave to cool for 15 minutes.

Pour the coconut mixture into a blender and blend for 30 seconds. It will NOT be smooth. DO NOT CONTINUE TO BLEND TO GET TO SMOOTH – it will never happen. Trust me.

Turn the blender to low speed, and while the blender is running, add the guar gum by tapping it through the opening in the lid, and blend for 30 seconds.

Pour the ice cream custard into a bowl or jar, cover, and place in the 'fridge for at least 8 hours, but preferably overnight. Don't skip the chillin', no matter which type of churner you have.

Stir the chilled custard well to make sure it is completely mixed and read the churning and freezing section on page 23. Freeze the custard in your churner according to the manufacturer's instructions. It typically takes between 15 - 20 minutes to freeze to a soft-serve consistency.

Once the ice cream has frozen to a soft-serve consistency in the churner, add the remaining 2 oz. / 55g toasted frozen coconut flakes and churn until mixed through.

Quickly transfer the ice cream from the churning bowl into your pre-chilled container, cover, and place in the freezer for at least 8 hours, preferably overnight.

~~~~~~

Sneaky emergency rescue tip: Coconut meat can be funny stuff. If you see your ice cream custard looking like it is curdling, add an extra ½ tsp. of guar gum, and whack the blender on high for a few seconds. Oh, and don't panic. It will churn just fine.

Lavender Caramel Surprise Ice Cream

1 cup / 8 fl oz. heavy cream (see page 12)

1 cup / 8 fl oz. hemp milk, unsweetened (see page 12)

3 oz. / 100g xylitol (NO substitutes!)

½ tsp. sea salt

¼ oz. / 7g food grade dried lavender flowers

1 cup / 8 fl oz. thick coconut milk (see page 11)

1 tsp. guar gum

Caramel Toasted Pine Nuts (recipe page 92) this needs to be made & chilled in advance

Warm the cream, hemp milk, xylitol, and sea salt in a medium pan until it just starts to boil. Simmer for 1 minute, remove from the heat, stir in the lavender flowers, cover and leave to steep for an hour.

Strain the infused cream through a sieve to remove the lavender flowers.

Carefully pour the lavender-infused cream mixture into a blender, add the thick coconut milk and blend for 10 seconds.

Turn the blender to low speed, and while the blender is running, add the guar gum by tapping it through the opening in the lid, and blend for 30 seconds.

Pour the ice cream custard into a bowl or jar, cover, and place in the 'fridge for at least 8 hours, but preferably overnight. Don't skip the chillin', no matter which type of churner you have.

Stir the chilled custard well to make sure it is completely mixed and read the churning and freezing section on page 23. Freeze the custard in your churner according to the manufacturer's instructions. It typically takes between 15 - 20 minutes to freeze to a soft-serve consistency.

Once the ice cream has frozen to a soft-serve consistency in the churner, pour the frozen caramel toasted pine nuts through the opening in the top of the churner and churn until mixed through.

Quickly transfer it from the churning bowl into your pre-chilled container, and place in the freezer for at least 8 hours, preferably overnight.

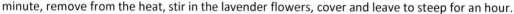

I have resisted anything and everything lavender since time began. Lavender reminds me of aging ladies, because it always seemed to be the preferred scent in lotions and potions of older ladies in England. I don't know if that's still true. And then Tina asked me to make Lavender Ice Cream, and since I love Tina, I obliged. I am now entirely smitten with lavender. And, oh! those caramel toasted pine nuts! I dare you to not eat them all before they get in the ice cream.

Dirty Hippie Ice Cream

1 ¾ cups / 14 fl oz. thin coconut milk, unsweetened (see page 11)

3 ½ oz. / 100g xylitol (NO substitutes!)

4 chai teabags

1 ¾ cups / 14 fl oz. heavy cream (see page 12)

1 ½ TBSP espresso powder

½ tsp. sea salt

1 tsp. guar gum

Warm the thin coconut milk and xylitol in a medium pan until it just starts to boil. Remove from the heat, add the chai teabags, stir well and leave for an hour to steep.

Pour the chai-infused milk through a sieve to remove the teabags, and then return the infused milk to the pan over a low heat.

Add the cream, espresso powder, and sea salt and stir well until the espresso powder is dissolved, and then remove from the heat.

Carefully pour the espresso chai mixture into a blender and blend for 10 seconds.

Turn the blender to low speed, and while the blender is running, add the guar gum by tapping it through the opening in the lid, and blend for 30 seconds.

Pour the ice cream custard into a bowl or jar, cover, and place in the 'fridge for at least 8 hours, but preferably overnight. Don't skip the chillin', no matter which type of churner you have.

Stir the chilled custard well to make sure it is completely mixed and read the churning and freezing section on page 23. Freeze the custard in your churner according to the manufacturer's instructions. It typically takes between 15 - 20 minutes to freeze to a soft-serve consistency.

Once the ice cream has frozen to a soft-serve consistency, quickly transfer it from the churning bowl into your pre-chilled container, and place in the freezer for at least 8 hours, preferably overnight.

~~~~~~

What's a Dirty Hippie? Also known as a Dirty Chai, a Dirty Hippie is a Chai Latte with 2 shots of espresso in. A Dirty Hippie with Whipped Cream is my favorite coffee shop treat. As long as it's made with heavy cream and no sugar, of course. I had to see if I could recreate the magic in ice cream form, so if you've never had a Dirty Hippie Latte, you can experience it in its frozen state right in the comfort of your own home. And if you're familiar with the gloriousness that is the Dirty Hippie Latte, you're gonna fall head over heels for this cold and creamy dish of YUM.

You may not be counting, but I thought I should mention that there's 15 different ice creams in this cookbook that involve nuts. That's around a third of the book. Unless you count coconut milk in that, in which case it's just about the entire book. So, let's talk about nuts for a few minutes, because clearly nuts are important. And because really, nuts are stinkin' awesome. And, on a ketogenic diet, nuts are a sure tasty way to include some fantastic whole-food fats in the proceedings.

Nuts, nuts, nuts. I've always been a big nut fan. I blame my father. From my mother I inherited a desire to cook, a mind like a steel trap when managing the household budget, a sweet tooth, and a penchant for ironing everything – and I mean *everything* – that comes out of the washing machine. From my father I inherited mad driving skills, silky fine hair, a lifelong fascination with psychotherapy, and a love for nuts.

Over the years I've toasted them, chopped them, ground them, flaked them, and even burnt a few. Except no one likes burnt nuts. I believe I have mentioned that more than a couple of times in these pages. I maintain it is absolutely true.

Growing up, Christmas in England meant piles of nuts – at least at our house. All kinds of nuts from salted peanuts to sugared almonds; and masses of fresh nuts still in their hard, brown winter coats. Every Christmas Eve, out would come the nutcrackers and large wooden bowls brimming with unshelled nuts – brazils, walnuts, cobnuts (hazelnuts), and almonds. As a family we sure put those nutcrackers through their paces, but mostly it was my father and I who took first place in the nut-cracking and devouring stakes. If I had to pick a favorite, though, it wouldn't be hard. Hazelnuts all the way, baby!

Way back when, in London, and Perth, Australia – when I was a professional Chocolatier – as well as being up to my elbows in liquid chocolate every day, I used to roast hazelnuts by hand over an open flame. We were artisans, you know. None of this store-bought pre-roasted debauchery. I'd pile the nuts into a round metal drum and snap shut the little flap on top. The drum then sat on a metal stand which straddled an open flame, and it had a wooden handle at one end. I would sit on a stool and slowly turn that dented, flame-scorched drum by hand until those hazels were a deep, even, golden brown right the way through; by Jove those were the best tasting nuts I have ever had the pleasure of popping into my mouth. Then we'd drench them in dark, glistening chocolate. Oh, yes.

These days my hazelnut roasting episodes aren't nearly as winsome or romantic as in times past, but a roasted hazelnut is still a roasted hazelnut when it comes down to the eating. My only issue with roasting hazelnuts is how to not eat them all 4 seconds after they've cooled down. In the Nutty Vanilla Fudge Ice Cream I started out with 4 oz. but there was only 3 oz. left by the time churning commenced. I don't think I can get away with blaming that one on the "kids". Have you ever met a cat that likes roasted hazelnuts?

I rest my case. Guilty as charged.

White Russian On The Rocks Ice Cream

1 ¼ cups / 10 fl oz. almond milk, unsweetened vanilla

1 ¾ oz. / 50g xylitol (NO substitutes!)

5 TBSP Kahlua

1 ¾ cups / 14 fl oz. heavy cream (see page 12)

½ cup / 4 fl oz. avocado oil

1 tsp. vanilla extract

1 tsp. guar gum

Warm the almond milk, xylitol, and Kahlua in a medium pan until it just starts to boil. Simmer for 1 minute and remove from the heat.

Place the cream, avocado oil, and vanilla extract in a blender with the warm Kahlua milk, and blend on low for 30 seconds.

With the blender still on low speed, and while the blender is running, add the guar gum by tapping it through the opening in the lid, and blend for 30 seconds.

Pour the ice cream custard into a bowl or jar, cover, and place in the 'fridge for at least 8 hours, but preferably overnight. Don't skip the chillin', no matter which type of churner you have.

Stir the chilled custard well to make sure it is completely mixed and read the churning and freezing section on page 23. Freeze the custard in your churner according to the manufacturer's instructions. It typically takes between 15 - 20 minutes to freeze to a soft-serve consistency.

Once the ice cream has frozen to a soft-serve consistency, quickly transfer it from the churning bowl into your pre-chilled container, and place in the freezer for at least 8 hours, preferably overnight.

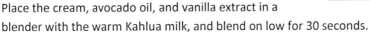

This was a request from both Mrs. Ketovangelist and the ever-awesome Mandy Pagano, who blogs over at www.ketovangelist.com, as well as being a kick-a** KETO Coach. I was more than happy to oblige, although I had to study up on what a White Russian was. I left out the vodka since it adds only alcohol and no flavor, and I cooked the Kahlua so there'd be no getting drunk on ice cream.

If you want the alcohol kick, add it right at the end – after the guar gum and before the chilling. You will still need to heat the almond milk and xylitol up though, in case you thought the only reason for the heating was to drive the alcohol off.

This ice cream is incredibly smooth and creamy, so with or without the kick it's delightful.

Nutty Vanilla Fudge Ice Cream

3 oz. / 85g hazelnuts, toasted

1 cup / 8 fl oz. heavy cream (see page 12)

1 ½ cup / 12 fl oz. almond milk, unsweetened vanilla

3 ½ oz. / 100g xylitol (NO substitutes!)

1 tsp. sea salt

1 ½ cup / 12 fl oz. thick coconut milk (see page 11)

2 tsp. vanilla extract

1 tsp. guar gum

½ batch Chocolate Fudge Ripple (recipe page 87) this
needs to be made in advance

Chop the toasted hazelnuts roughly and store in an airtight
container in the freezer.

Warm the cream, almond milk, xylitol, and sea salt in a medium pan until it just starts to boil.
Simmer for 1 minute, then remove from the heat and cool for 15 minutes.

Carefully pour the cream mixture into a blender, add the thick coconut milk and vanilla extract
and blend for 10 seconds.

Turn the blender to low speed, and while the blender is running, add the guar gum by tapping it
through the opening in the lid, and blend for 30 seconds.

Pour the ice cream custard into a bowl or jar, cover, and place in the 'fridge for at least 8 hours,
but preferably overnight. Don't skip the chillin', no matter which type of churner you have.

Stir the chilled custard well to make sure it is completely mixed and read the churning and
freezing section on page 23. Freeze the custard in your churner according to the manufacturer's
instructions. It typically takes between 15 - 20 minutes to freeze to a soft-serve consistency.

Once the ice cream has frozen to a soft-serve consistency in the churner, pour the frozen
chopped nuts through the opening in the top of the churner and churn until mixed through.

Once the nuts are mixed through, quickly spoon a layer of ice cream into the bottom of your cold
storage container. Spoon large dollops of Chocolate Fudge Sauce over the ice cream, and then
continue to layer ice cream and sauce until the ice cream has all been removed from the churner.
Be careful to 'dollop' the ice cream layer over the sauce so that there is as little movement of the
sauce as possible. Otherwise you will get 'muddy' ice cream.

Cover the container and place in the freezer for at least 8 hours, preferably overnight.

Peppermint Choc Chip Ice Cream

1 ¼ cup / 10 fl oz. thin coconut milk (see page 11)

1 ½ oz. / 40g fresh mint leaves

1 ¼ cup / 10 fl oz. heavy cream (see page 12)

½ tsp. sea salt

4 oz. / 100g xylitol (NO substitutes!)

1 cup / 8 fl oz. thick coconut milk (see page 11)

1 tsp. guar gum

1 ½ oz. / 45g cocoa nibs, chilled

Place thin coconut milk, mint leaves, cream, sea salt, and xylitol in a pan, stir well and bring just to the boil. Remove from the heat, cover and leave to steep for an hour.

Sieve the milk mixture to remove the mint leaves, pressing the mint leaves against the sieve to remove as much flavor as possible.

Place the mint milk and thick coconut milk in the blender and blend for 10 seconds.

Turn the blender to low speed, and while the blender is running, add the guar gum by tapping it through the opening in the lid, and blend for 30 seconds.

Pour the ice cream custard into a bowl or jar, cover, and place in the 'fridge for at least 8 hours, but preferably overnight. Don't skip the chillin', no matter which type of churner you have.

Stir the chilled custard well to make sure it is completely mixed and read the churning and freezing section on page 23. Freeze the custard in your churner according to the manufacturer's instructions. It typically takes between 15 - 20 minutes to freeze to a soft-serve consistency.

Once the ice cream has frozen to a soft-serve consistency in the churner, pour the chilled cocoa nibs through the opening in the top of the churner and churn until mixed through.

Quickly transfer the ice cream from the churning bowl into your pre-chilled container, cover, and place in the freezer for at least 8 hours, preferably overnight.

~~~~~~

Sneaky money-saving tip: If you're going to make any quantity of this most delicious and refreshing of ice creams, I'd start growing your own mint. I planted a $1.50 shoot in a large pot, and 6 weeks later had enough mint to open a mint farm. Fresh mint also makes delicious Mint Tea, which is a god-send if you don't like drinking plain water or green tea as much as I don't.

Ballistic Coffee Ice Cream

1 ¼ cup / 10 fl oz. almond milk, unsweetened vanilla

3 ¼ oz. / 90g xylitol (NO substitutes!)

½ tsp. sea salt

1 cup / 8 fl oz. heavy cream (see page 12)

¾ cup / 6 fl oz. thick coconut milk (see page 11)

½ cup / 4 fl oz. MCT oil

2 TBSP espresso powder

½ tsp. guar gum

Chocolate Macadamias Nuts (recipe page 92) – this needs to be made and frozen in advance

Place the almond milk, xylitol, sea salt, cream, thick coconut milk, MCT oil, and espresso powder in a blender and blend on low for 30 seconds.

With the blender still on low speed, and while the blender is running, add the guar gum by tapping it through the opening in the lid, and blend for 30 seconds.

Pour the ice cream custard into a bowl or jar, cover, and place in the 'fridge for at least 8 hours, but preferably overnight. Don't skip the chillin', no matter which type of churner you have.

Stir the chilled custard well to make sure it is completely mixed and read the churning and freezing section on page 23. Freeze the custard in your churner according to the manufacturer's instructions. It typically takes between 15 – 20 minutes to freeze to a soft-serve consistency.

Once the ice cream has frozen to a soft-serve consistency, quickly transfer it from the churning bowl into your pre-chilled container and stir the chocolate macadamias through as fast as you can. Cover and place in the freezer for at least 8 hours, preferably overnight.

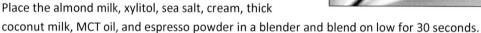

Of all the coffee ice creams in this cookbook, this one is *by far* my favorite. It started as another of Brian Williamson's bright ideas.

"Make me coffee ice cream with macadamia nuts in it," he said. *"And if that's not enough of a challenge, dip the macadamias in chocolate."*

Oh, OK then. And because my brain is not the kind that can let food and kitchen challenges go easily, I off toddled to break out the dipping forks and see if I could persuade sugar-free chocolate to wrap itself around macadamias and not freeze so hard it broke teeth.

I made it hardcore KETO with the addition of MCT oil, so it's essentially a frozen version of your morning cuppa plus the king of KETO nuts and 100% chocolate thrown in for giggles.

Sinless Cinnamon Ice Cream

1 ½ cup / 12 fl oz. almond milk, unsweetened vanilla

1 cup / 8 fl oz. heavy cream (see page 12)

3 ½ oz. / 100g xylitol (NO substitutes!)

½ tsp. sea salt

1 cup / 8 fl oz. thick coconut milk (see page 11)

1 ½ tsp. ground cinnamon

¼ tsp. vanilla extract

1 tsp. guar gum

Place the almond milk, cream, xylitol, sea salt, thick coconut milk, ground cinnamon, and vanilla extract into a blender and blend for 10 seconds.

Turn the blender to low speed, and while the blender is running, add the guar gum by tapping it through the opening in the lid, and blend for 30 seconds.

Pour the ice cream custard into a bowl or jar, cover, and place in the 'fridge for at least 8 hours, but preferably overnight. Don't skip the chillin', no matter which type of churner you have.

Stir the chilled custard well to make sure it is completely mixed and read the churning and freezing section on page 23. Freeze the custard in your churner according to the manufacturer's instructions. It typically takes between 15 - 20 minutes to freeze to a soft-serve consistency.

Once the ice cream has frozen to a soft-serve consistency, quickly transfer it from the churning bowl into your pre-chilled container, and place in the freezer for at least 8 hours, preferably overnight.

~~~~~~

The British aren't really Cinnamon Hounds like the Americans are, but I figured that what with the Stars and Stripes Lovers' allegiance to Snickerdoodle Cookies, and their addiction to Cinnamon Rolls, I was probably onto a winner with Cinnamon Ice Cream. During the taste-tests all everyone wanted to know was how I had made ice cream taste like cookies and rolls, which is a really, really good thing if you are gluten-, grain-, and sugar-free and can't eat them live and direct.

To my complete surprise this rose straight into my Top 3 favorite ice cream flavors. Who knew that the girl from Limey Land would one day be swept off her feet by a few dusty brown sticks? America, I think you're onto something.

Lemon Pop Ice Cream

1 ¼ cup / 10 fl oz. thin coconut milk (see page 11)

4 oz. / 110g xylitol (NO substitutes!)

½ tsp. sea salt

¾ cup / 6 fl oz. heavy cream (see page 12)

Zest of 3 whole lemons

8 oz. / 225g crème fraiche

½ cup / 4 fl oz. thick coconut milk (see page 11)

1 TBSP lemon juice

½ oz. / 15g poppy seeds

1 tsp. guar gum

Warm the thin coconut milk, xylitol, sea salt, and cream in a medium pan until it just starts to boil. Remove from the heat, add the lemon zest, cover and leave for an hour to steep.

Pour the lemon-infused milk through a sieve to remove the zest.

Place the crème fraiche and thick coconut milk in a blender with the lemon-infused milk, and the lemon juice, and blend for 10 seconds.

Turn the blender to low speed, and while the blender is running, add the poppy seeds followed by the guar gum by tapping them through the opening in the lid, and blend for 30 seconds.

Pour the ice cream custard into a bowl or jar, cover, and place in the 'fridge for at least 8 hours, but preferably overnight. Don't skip the chillin', no matter which type of churner you have.

Stir the chilled custard well to make sure it is completely mixed and read the churning and freezing section on page 23. Freeze the custard in your churner according to the manufacturer's instructions. It typically takes between 15 – 20 minutes to freeze to a soft-serve consistency.

Once the ice cream has frozen to a soft-serve consistency, quickly transfer it from the churning bowl into your pre-chilled container, and place in the freezer for at least 8 hours, preferably overnight.

~~~~~~

So refreshing on a hot day, this creamy smooth lemon ice cream will brighten up the hottest afternoon. Or morning. Evening, too.

This is not a pucker-up-Buttercup ice cream, it's more of a deep, but gentle lemon, with the added crunch of poppy seeds. It's beautiful. Lemons are my favorite.

Triple X Zone Ice Cream (*uses eggs)

1 cup / 8 fl oz. hemp milk, unsweetened (see page 12)

1 cup / 8 fl oz. heavy cream (see page 12)

4 ½ oz. / 100g xylitol (NO substitutes!)

½ tsp. sea salt

1 oz. / 30g raw, unsweetened cocoa powder

1 ½ oz. / 40g 100% unsweetened chocolate, chopped

1 cup / 8 fl oz. thick coconut milk (see page 11)

1 tsp. vanilla extract

½ tsp. guar gum

Chocolate Fudge Ripple (recipe page 87) – this needs to be made in advance

Chocolate Fudge Brownies (recipe page 98) – this needs to be made and frozen in advance

Place the hemp milk, cream, xylitol, sea salt, and cocoa powder in a pan over medium heat and whisk until the cocoa powder is completely mixed in. Bring to the boil, reduce the heat, and simmer for 1 minute, whisking constantly.

Remove pan from the heat and stir in the chopped chocolate. Leave to cool for 15 minutes, stirring well occasionally. Place the thick coconut milk and vanilla extract in the blender, add the cooled chocolate custard and blend for 10 seconds.

Turn the blender to low speed, and while the blender is running, add the guar gum by tapping it through the opening in the lid, and blend for 30 seconds.

Pour the ice cream custard into a bowl or jar, cover, and place in the 'fridge for at least 8 hours, but preferably overnight. Don't skip the chillin', no matter which type of churner you have.

Stir the chilled custard well to make sure it is completely mixed and read the churning and freezing section on page 23. Freeze the custard in your churner according to the manufacturer's instructions. It typically takes between 15 - 20 minutes to freeze to a soft-serve consistency.

Once the ice cream has frozen to a soft-serve consistency in the churner, quickly spoon a layer of ice cream into the bottom of your cold storage container. Put Brownie Bites and dollops of Chocolate Fudge Ripple on the ice cream, and then continue to layer ice cream, brownie bites, and chocolate ripple until the ice cream has all been removed from the churner.

Cover and place in the freezer for at least 8 hours, preferably overnight.

Yes. KETO brownies that stay soft and chewy in the freezer: #WINNING

Vanilla Green Tea Ice Cream

1 ¼ cup / 10 fl oz. thin coconut milk (see page 11)

1 ¼ cup / 10 fl oz. heavy cream (see page 12)

3 ½ oz. / 100g xylitol (NO substitutes!)

½ tsp. sea salt

2 TBSP green tea powder / matcha powder

1 cup / 8 fl oz. thick coconut milk (see page 11)

3 tsp. vanilla extract

1 tsp. guar gum

Warm the thin coconut milk, cream, xylitol, and sea salt in a medium pan until it just starts to boil. Simmer for 1 minute, then remove from the heat and cool for 5 minutes.

Vigorously whisk the green tea powder into the hot cream mixture until it is completely dissolved.

Carefully pour the warm green tea cream into a blender, add the thick coconut milk and vanilla extract and blend for 10 seconds.

Turn the blender to low speed, and while the blender is running, add the guar gum by tapping it through the opening in the lid, and blend for 30 seconds.

Pour the ice cream custard into a bowl or jar, cover, and place in the 'fridge for at least 8 hours, but preferably overnight. Don't skip the chillin', no matter which type of churner you have.

Stir the chilled custard well to make sure it is completely mixed and read the churning and freezing section on page 23. Freeze the custard in your churner according to the manufacturer's instructions. It typically takes between 15 - 20 minutes to freeze to a soft-serve consistency.

Once the ice cream has frozen to a soft-serve consistency, quickly transfer it from the churning bowl into your pre-chilled container, and place in the freezer for at least 8 hours, preferably overnight.

~~~~~~

I dislike the taste of green tea intensely, so you may wonder why I made y'all a Green Tea Ice Cream. When I asked you lovely people on Facebook what new ice cream flavors you wanted there was a resounding cry for some matcha in your lives. So here we are. I had to call in an extra bunch of green tea lovers to taste test it, because no matter what I did to it, I couldn't make my taste buds get on board. The taste testers, however, loved it.

Green tea is fantastically good for you, so if you love the flavor, here's a new way to get some in.

Peanut Butter Ice Cream

2 cups / 16 fl oz. hemp milk, unsweetened (see page 12)

¾ cup / 6 fl oz. smooth natural unsweetened peanut butter

6 ¼ oz. / 175g xylitol (NO substitutes!)

½ tsp. sea salt

½ cup / 4 fl oz. heavy cream (see page 12)

¼ tsp. vanilla extract

½ tsp. guar gum

Place the hemp milk, peanut butter, xylitol, sea salt, cream, and vanilla extract into a blender and blend for 10 seconds.

Turn the blender to low speed, and while the blender is running, add the guar gum by tapping it through the opening in the lid, and blend for 30 seconds.

Pour the ice cream custard into a bowl or jar, cover, and place in the 'fridge for at least 8 hours, but preferably overnight. Don't skip the chillin', no matter which type of churner you have.

Stir the chilled custard well to make sure it is completely mixed and read the churning and freezing section on page 23. Freeze the custard in your churner according to the manufacturer's instructions. It typically takes between 15 - 20 minutes to freeze to a soft-serve consistency.

Once the ice cream has frozen to a soft-serve consistency, quickly transfer it from the churning bowl into your pre-chilled container, cover, and place in the freezer for at least 8 hours, preferably overnight.

~~~~~~

Here's a few of the comments from my blog about this recipe:

Ellen said, "YUM.....JUST YUM! What an incredible ice cream! LOVE it!! It is DEFINITELY a '5' star recipe!!!"

Suzie said, "Made this ice cream this weekend... It was awesome – way easy to make, the recipe really worked. Thank you, Carrie Brown!!! "

Deb said, "Love, love, love this ice cream. Getting ready to make another batch. "

NOTE: KETO is about more than just very low carb. It's also about reducing inflammation so that you can truly thrive. Some people find peanuts inflammatory. If this is you, then we recommend that you avoid eating them, however much you love them.

You can sub with Almond Butter if you can't or don't want to do Peanut Butter.

Maple Bacon Crack Ice Cream

1 ½ cups / 12 fl oz. heavy cream (see page 12)

1 ½ cup / 12 fl oz. hemp milk, unsweetened (see page 12)

3 oz. / 85g xylitol (NO substitutes!)

2 ½ TBSP maple extract

½ tsp. sea salt

1 cup / 8 fl oz. thick coconut milk (see page 11)

1 tsp. guar gum

Bacon Ripple (recipe page 88) – this needs to be made in advance

Warm the cream, hemp milk, xylitol, maple extract, and sea salt in a medium pan until it just starts to boil. Simmer for 1 minute, then remove from the heat and cool for 15 minutes.

Carefully pour the cream mixture into a blender, add the thick coconut milk and blend for 10 seconds.

Turn the blender to low speed, and while the blender is running, add the guar gum by tapping it through the opening in the lid, and blend for 30 seconds.

Pour the ice cream custard into a bowl or jar, cover, and place in the 'fridge for at least 8 hours, but preferably overnight. Don't skip the chillin', no matter which type of churner you have.

Stir the chilled custard well to make sure it is completely mixed and read the churning and freezing section on page 23. Freeze the custard in your churner according to the manufacturer's instructions. It typically takes between 15 - 20 minutes to freeze to a soft-serve consistency.

Once the ice cream has frozen to a soft-serve consistency, quickly spoon a layer of ice cream into the bottom of your cold storage container. Spoon dollops of Bacon Ripple over the ice cream, and then continue to layer ice cream and bacon ripple until the ice cream has all been removed from the churner. Be careful to dollop the ice cream and not stir. You don't want "muddy" ice cream.

Cover and place in the freezer for at least 8 hours, preferably overnight.

~~~~~~

I blame Brian Williamson for this Bacon Ripple *thang.* A text about BBQ Sauce spawned a new Maple Bacon BBQ Sauce which blew the doors off for every Texan that tasted it. The excitement got me thinking about other uses. It was a short hop from there to a bacon ripple for ice cream. After I created the ripple I am not sure how there was any left to use, but somehow enough remained uneaten for me to photograph it. YES. There's a soft ripple of bacon in your ice cream.

Orange Creamsicle Ice Cream

Zest of 4 oranges

1 cup / 8 fl oz. almond milk, unsweetened vanilla

½ cup / 4 fl oz. heavy cream (see page 12)

3 ½ oz. / 100g xylitol (NO substitutes!)

½ tsp. sea salt

1 cup / 8 fl oz. thick coconut milk (see page 11)

½ tsp. vanilla extract

1 tsp. orange extract

1 tsp. guar gum

Sugar-free Marshmallows (recipe page 94) – these need to be made in advance

Zest the oranges directly into a small pan. Let your children eat the oranges. Or your non-KETO spouse. The cat? The dog? Maybe the neighbor.

Add the almond milk, cream, xylitol, and sea salt to the pan with the zest, stir well, and bring just to the boil. Remove from the heat, cover, and leave to cool.

Pass the orange milk through a sieve to remove the zest. Discard the zest.

Place the orange milk in a blender with the thick coconut milk, vanilla extract, and orange extract, and blend for 10 seconds.

Turn the blender to low speed, and while the blender is running, add the guar gum by tapping it through the opening in the lid, and blend for 30 seconds.

Pour the ice cream custard into a bowl or jar, cover, and place in the 'fridge for at least 8 hours, but preferably overnight. Don't skip the chillin', no matter which type of churner you have.

Stir the chilled custard well to make sure it is completely mixed and read the churning and freezing section on page 23. Freeze the custard in your churner according to the manufacturer's instructions. It typically takes between 15 - 20 minutes to freeze to a soft-serve consistency.

Once the ice cream has frozen to a soft-serve consistency in the churner, quickly spoon a layer of ice cream into the bottom of your cold storage container. Sprinkle Marshmallows over the ice cream, and then continue to layer ice cream and Marshmallows until the ice cream has all been removed from the churner.

Cover and place in the freezer for at least 8 hours, preferably overnight.

PSL Bandwagon Ice Cream

1 cup / 8 fl oz. heavy cream (see page 12)

¾ cup / 6 fl oz. hemp milk, unsweetened (see page 12)

4 oz. / 100g xylitol (NO substitutes!)

½ tsp. sea salt

1 TBSP espresso powder

¾ cup / 6 fl oz. thick coconut milk (see page 11)

6 oz. / 170g pumpkin puree, plain unsweetened

½ tsp. ground cinnamon

1/8 tsp. ground ginger

1/8 tsp. ground clove

1/8 tsp. ground nutmeg

1 tsp. vanilla extract

1 tsp. guar gum

Warm the cream, hemp milk, xylitol, sea salt, and espresso powder in a medium pan until it just starts to boil. Simmer for 1 minute, then remove from the heat and leave to cool for 10 minutes.

Place the thick coconut milk, pumpkin puree, cinnamon, ginger, clove, nutmeg, and vanilla extract in a blender with the warm espresso cream, and blend until the custard is very smooth.

Turn the blender to low speed, and while the blender is running, add the guar gum by tapping it through the opening in the lid, and blend for 30 seconds.

Pour the ice cream custard into a bowl or jar, cover, and place in the 'fridge for at least 8 hours, but preferably overnight. Don't skip the chillin', no matter which type of churner you have.

Stir the chilled custard well to make sure it is completely mixed and read the churning and freezing section on page 23. Freeze the custard in your churner according to the manufacturer's instructions. It typically takes between 15 - 20 minutes to freeze to a soft-serve consistency.

Once the ice cream has frozen to a soft-serve consistency, quickly transfer it from the churning bowl into your pre-chilled container, and place in the freezer for at least 8 hours, preferably overnight.

~~~~~~

Pumpkin Spice Latte is probably the craziest food trend to descend on Americans all year. Every year there is yet One. More. Thing. made with this ubiquitous combination of flavors. Having grown up without pumpkin I have managed to evade the whole PSL thing for years. I am not typically a trend-follower. This year, I gave in and made you PSL Ice Cream. And it is awesome!

Coconut Fudge Chip Ice Cream

3 oz. / 85g flaked or desiccated coconut, unsweetened

1 ¼ cup / 10 fl oz. thin coconut milk (see page 11)

¾ cup / 6 fl oz. heavy cream (see page 12)

3 ½ oz. / 100g xylitol (NO substitutes!)

½ tsp. sea salt

1 ½ cups / 12 fl oz. thick coconut milk (see page 11)

1 tsp. guar gum

1 ¼ oz. / 35g cocoa nibs, chilled

½ batch Chocolate Fudge Ripple (recipe page 87) – this needs to be made in advance

Spread the coconut on a baking sheet and toast under a broiler (grill) until lightly browned. Browning happens very quickly – do not walk away! Remove from under the broiler (grill) and leave to cool.

Place toasted coconut, thin coconut milk, cream, xylitol, and sea salt, in a pan, and heat until it starts to boil. Remove from the heat, cover, and leave to cool.

Pour the coconut milk through a sieve to remove the toasted coconut. Press hard on the toasted coconut in the sieve to extract as much of the coconut juice as possible. You are not trying to press the coconut through the sieve, just trying to remove maximum amount of juice and flavor from it. Reserve the coconut meat for another use – add it to green smoothies or make the Orange Coconut Cupcakes over at www.carriebrown.com. They are delicious!

Place the pressed coconut milk in a blender with the thick coconut milk, and blend for 10 seconds.

Turn the blender to low speed, and while the blender is running, add the guar gum by tapping it through the opening in the lid, and blend for 30 seconds.

Pour the ice cream custard into a bowl or jar, cover, and place in the 'fridge for at least 8 hours, but preferably overnight. Don't skip the chillin', no matter which type of churner you have.

Stir the chilled custard well to make sure it is completely mixed and read the churning and freezing section on page 23. Freeze the custard in your churner according to the manufacturer's instructions. It typically takes between 15 - 20 minutes to freeze to a soft-serve consistency.

Once the ice cream has frozen to a soft-serve consistency in the churner, add the chilled cocoa nibs to the churner through the opening in the top, and churn until mixed through.

Once the nibs are mixed through, quickly spoon a layer of ice cream into the bottom of your cold storage container. Spoon large dollops of Chocolate Fudge Ripple over the ice cream, and then continue to layer ice cream and fudge until the ice cream has all been removed from the churner. Be careful to 'dollop" the ice cream layer over the Chocolate Fudge Ripple so that there is as little movement of the fudge as possible. Otherwise you will get 'muddy' ice cream.

Cover and place in the freezer for at least 8 hours, preferably overnight.

~~~~~~

If you're wondering why there are 3 different coconut ice creams going on around here, you can mostly blame The Internet. Coconut is everywhere! Coconut is also extraordinarily good for us, and health gurus across the globe never miss an opportunity to remind me of its umpteen virtues. KETO folks just love the stuff. Coconut oil, coconut milk, coconut cream, plain old coconut meat, coconut butter. (Just don't eat coconut sugar – it's no different than regular sugar.)

The first coconut ice cream I developed – the tantalizing Toasted Triple Coconut – was made entirely with hardcore coconut lovers in mind. I packed as much of that glorious white stuff into it as I could muster. It is lumpy, bumpy and chock full of tender, juicy coconut meat. If you love ice cream with some serious texture going on, this one's for you.

The second one was inspired by a lovely reader – adding some bright, zesty lime to the proceedings. It also felt rather tropical, a bit like a Piña Colada without the booze. OK, and without the pineapple, but you get the idea. I decided to make this one a little less lumpy and bumpy, but it's still all-coconut, all the time.

The third one I created for all you smooth-and-creamy ice cream lovers. Why should you miss out on all the coconutty goodness just because you don't care for bumpy bits? Except then I turned around and added cocoa nibs. I know, right? But you see, you asked for Coconut Chip Ice Cream, and having 4 coconut ice creams in one book seemed a little much. The good news is that if you really, really just want super-silky, creamy, dreamy coconut ice cream, you can just leave the cocoa nibs out and truly get your smooth on.

Everyone wins!

Lime In The Coconut Ice Cream

3 oz. / 85g flaked or desiccated coconut, unsweetened

Zest of 2 limes

¾ cup / 6 fl oz. thin coconut milk (see page 11)

¾ cup / 6 fl oz. heavy cream (see page 12)

½ tsp. sea salt

3 ½ oz. / 100g xylitol (NO substitutes!)

1 ½ cups / 12 fl oz. thick coconut milk (see page 11)

1 tsp. guar gum

Spread the coconut on a baking sheet and toast under a broiler (grill) until lightly browned. Browning happens very quickly – do not walk away! Remove from under the broiler (grill) and leave to cool.

Zest the limes directly into a small pan.

Add the thin coconut milk, cream, sea salt, and xylitol to the lime zest in the pan and bring just to the boil. Remove from the heat, cover, and leave to cool.

Pass the lime milk through a sieve to remove the zest. Set zest to one side and reserve. You will use it at the churning stage.

Place the lime milk in a blender with the thick coconut milk and toasted coconut, and blend for 10 seconds. It will NOT be smooth. Don't try to make it be smooth!

Turn the blender to low speed, and while the blender is running, add the guar gum by tapping it through the opening in the lid, and blend for 30 seconds.

Pour the ice cream custard into a bowl or jar, cover, and place in the 'fridge for at least 8 hours, but preferably overnight. Don't skip the chillin', no matter which type of churner you have.

Stir the chilled custard well to make sure it is completely mixed and read the churning and freezing section on page 23. Freeze the custard in your churner according to the manufacturer's instructions. It typically takes between 15 - 20 minutes to freeze to a soft-serve consistency.

Once the ice cream has frozen to a soft-serve consistency in the churner, add the lime zest to the churner through the opening in the top, and churn until mixed through.

Quickly transfer the ice cream from the churning bowl into your pre-chilled container, cover, and place in the freezer for at least 8 hours, preferably overnight.

Nutty Mud Puddle Ice Cream

4 oz. / 110g toasted hazelnuts

1 cup / 8 fl oz. almond milk, unsweetened vanilla

1 cup / 8 fl oz. heavy cream (see page 12)

3 ½ oz. / 100g xylitol (NO substitutes!)

2 tsps. glycerin

½ tsp. sea salt

2 oz. / 55g 100% cocoa solids chocolate (unsweetened), chopped

1 cup / 8 fl oz. thick coconut milk (see page 11)

1 tsp. vanilla extract

1 tsp. guar gum

Warm the hazelnuts, almond milk, cream, xylitol, glycerin and sea salt in a medium pan until it just starts to boil. Remove from the heat, cover and leave for an hour to steep. Soaking your nuts is important.

Rewarm the pan over a low heat, and once warm add the chopped chocolate and stir until completely melted. Carefully pour the warm chocolate hazelnut cream into a blender, add the thick coconut milk and vanilla extract and blend on high until smooth.

Turn the blender to low speed, and while the blender is running, add the guar gum by tapping it through the opening in the lid, and blend for 30 seconds.

Pour the ice cream custard into a bowl or jar, cover, and place in the 'fridge for at least 8 hours, but preferably overnight. Don't skip the chillin', no matter which type of churner you have.

Stir the chilled custard well to make sure it is completely mixed and read the churning and freezing section on page 23. Freeze the custard in your churner according to the manufacturer's instructions. It typically takes between 15 - 20 minutes to freeze to a soft-serve consistency.

Once the ice cream has frozen to a soft-serve consistency, quickly transfer it from the churning bowl into your pre-chilled container, and place in the freezer for at least 8 hours, preferably overnight.

~~~~~~

Hands up anyone who doesn't like Nutella. *Carrie raises hand*

Don't get me wrong, I love the taste, but have you ever read the ingredients list on a jar of it? Ewwwwww. So, here's an ice cream version for you that has all the yum and none of the yuck.

Mighty Moose Tracks Ice Cream

1 ¼ cups / 10 fl oz. almond milk, unsweetened vanilla

3 ½ oz. / 100g xylitol (NO substitutes!)

1 tsp. sea salt

¾ cup / 6 fl oz. heavy cream (see page 12)

1 ½ cups / 12 fl oz. thick coconut milk (see page 11)

2 tsp. vanilla extract

1 tsp. guar gum

½ batch Chocolate Fudge Ripple (recipe page 87) – this needs to be made in advance

Peanut Butter Drops (recipe page 91 – this needs to be made and frozen in advance

Place all ingredients EXCEPT the guar gum in a blender, and blend for 10 seconds.

Turn the blender to low speed, and while the blender is running, add the guar gum by tapping it through the opening in the lid, and blend for 30 seconds.

Pour the ice cream custard into a bowl or jar, cover, and place in the 'fridge for at least 8 hours, but preferably overnight. Don't skip the chillin', no matter which type of churner you have.

Stir the chilled custard well to make sure it is completely mixed and read the churning and freezing section on page 23. Freeze the custard in your churner according to the manufacturer's instructions. It typically takes between 15 - 20 minutes to freeze to a soft-serve consistency.

Once the ice cream has frozen to a soft-serve consistency in the churner, quickly spoon a layer of ice cream into the bottom of your cold storage container. Spoon large dollops of Chocolate Fudge Ripple over the ice cream, then sprinkle Peanut Butter Drops on top. Continue to layer ice cream, Fudge Ripple, and Peanut Butter Drops until the ice cream has all been removed from the churner. Be careful to 'dollop' the ice cream layer over the Fudge Ripple so that there is as little movement of the fudge ripple as possible. Otherwise you will get 'muddy' ice cream.

Cover and place in the deep freezer for at least 8 hours, preferably overnight.

~~~~~~

I've always loved moose. I once saw 6 moose in the wild up in Canada one winter, and I was so excited I nearly fell out of the truck. I'm not entirely sure what the fudge ripple and peanut butter drops have to do with moose, but this stuff sure tastes good.

Lemon Meringue Pie Ice Cream (*uses eggs)

Zest of one lemon

1 cup / 8 fl oz. heavy cream (see page 12)

2 oz. / 65g xylitol (NO substitutes!)

½ tsp. sea salt

2 cups / 16 fl oz. Lemon Curd (recipe page 90) – this needs to be made in advance

½ cup / 4 fl oz. Greek yogurt

1 tsp. guar gum

Sugar-free Meringue Cookies (recipe page 95) – this needs to be made in advance

Lemon Shortbread Cookies (recipe page 96) – this needs to be made in advance & chilled

Zest the lemon directly into a small pan.

Add the cream, xylitol, and sea salt to the pan with the lemon zest, stir well, and heat until bubbles just start to break the surface. Remove from the heat, cover and leave to cool.

Sieve the cooled lemon cream to remove the lemon zest. Discard the zest.

Place the lemon cream in a blender with the Lemon Curd and yogurt, and blend for 10 seconds.

Turn the blender to low speed, and while the blender is running, add the guar gum by tapping it through the opening in the lid, and blend for 30 seconds.

Pour the ice cream custard into a bowl or jar, cover, and place in the 'fridge for at least 8 hours, but preferably overnight. Don't skip the chillin', no matter which type of churner you have.

Stir the chilled custard well to make sure it is completely mixed and read the churning and freezing section on page 23. Freeze the custard in your churner according to the manufacturer's instructions. It typically takes between 15 - 20 minutes to freeze to a soft-serve consistency.

Once the ice cream has frozen to a soft-serve consistency in the churner, quickly spoon a layer into the bottom of your cold storage container. Sprinkle Meringue Cookies and chilled broken Lemon Shortbread Cookies over the ice cream. Continue to layer ice cream and cookies until the ice cream has all been removed from the churner.

Cover and place in the freezer for at least 8 hours, preferably overnight.

~~~~~~

Oh, for the love of all things lemony and delectable, this ice cream is ridiculous.

Root Beer Float Ice Cream

1 cup / 8 fl oz. thick coconut milk (see page 11)

1 ¼ cup / 10 fl oz. almond milk, vanilla unsweetened

½ cup / 4 fl oz. heavy cream (see page 12)

¼ cup / 2 fl oz. avocado oil

3 ½ oz. / 125g xylitol (NO substitutes!)

½ tsp. sea salt

1 tsp. vanilla extract

4 tsp. root beer extract

1 tsp. guar gum

Place all ingredients EXCEPT the guar gum in a blender and blend for 10 seconds.

Turn the blender to low speed, and while the blender is running, add the guar gum by tapping it through the opening in the lid, and blend for 30 seconds.

Pour the ice cream custard into a bowl or jar, cover, and place in the 'fridge for at least 8 hours, but preferably overnight. Don't skip the chillin', no matter which type of churner you have.

Stir the chilled custard well to make sure it is completely mixed and read the churning and freezing section on page 23. Freeze the custard in your churner according to the manufacturer's instructions. It typically takes between 15 - 20 minutes to freeze to a soft-serve consistency.

Once the ice cream has frozen to a soft-serve consistency, quickly transfer it from the churning bowl into your pre-chilled container, and place in the freezer for at least 8 hours, preferably overnight.

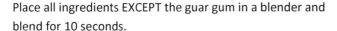

Sneaky laundry-saving tip: If you have never worked with root beer extract, it is the stain-iest stuff I have ever encountered. I thoroughly recommend wearing your oldest, grubbiest t-shirt while you're in the throes of making Root Beer Ice Cream, or root beer anything for that matter. Plus, save a kitchen countertop today! Wipe up any spills immediately!

I'd never had root beer until I landed on this side of the pond, but I quickly grew to love me a lovely, frothy root beer float. Now that I am a sugar-free zone, I had stopped partaking. Until now. Go on, pour some fizzy water over this Root Beer Ice Cream and have yourself a Root Beer Float. I dare you!

Frozen Mocha Cocoa Fudge Cheesecake

½ cup / 4 fl oz. hemp milk, unsweetened (see page 12)

¾ cup / 6 fl oz. heavy cream (see page 12)

4 ½ oz. / 125g xylitol (NO substitutes!)

½ tsp. sea salt

1 ½ oz. / 40g raw, unsweetened cocoa powder

1 oz. / 30g 100% cocoa solids chocolate (unsweetened), chopped

8 oz. / 225g full-fat cream cheese

½ cup / 4 fl oz. cold brew coffee concentrate

1 ¼ cups / 10 fl oz. sour cream

1 tsp. guar gum

Chocolate Crust (recipe page 98) – this needs to be made and frozen in advance

Place the hemp milk, cream, xylitol, sea salt, and cocoa powder in a pan over medium heat and whisk until the cocoa powder is completely mixed in. Bring to the boil, reduce the heat, and simmer for 1 minute, whisking constantly.

Remove pan from the heat and stir in the chopped chocolate until completely melted.

Place the cream cheese, cold brew coffee concentrate, and sour cream in a blender with the warm chocolate cream and blend on low for 30 seconds.

Turn the blender to low speed, and while the blender is running, add the guar gum by tapping it through the opening in the lid, and blend for 30 seconds.

Pour the ice cream custard into a bowl or jar, cover, and place in the 'fridge for at least 8 hours, but preferably overnight. Don't skip the chillin', no matter which type of churner you have.

Stir the chilled custard well to make sure it is completely mixed and read the churning and freezing section on page 23. Freeze the custard in your churner according to the manufacturer's instructions. It typically takes between 15 - 20 minutes to freeze to a soft-serve consistency.

Once the ice cream has frozen to a soft-serve consistency, quickly transfer it from the churning bowl and spread it evenly over the prepared chocolate crust. Cover and place in the freezer for at least 8 hours, preferably overnight.

Once frozen, remove from the pan, place on a cutting surface, and using a long serrated knife cut into squares using a sawing motion. You might find rinsing your knife with warm water and shaking the excess water off between cuts helps make it easier and / or the squares prettier. Place the squares in a container with parchment between the layers and store in the freezer.

Banana Cream Pie Ice Cream

1 cup / 8 fl oz. heavy cream (see page 12)

1 ¼ cups / 10 fl oz. almond milk, unsweetened vanilla

3 oz. / 100g xylitol (NO substitutes!)

4 tsps. banana extract

1 tsp. caramel extract

½ tsp. sea salt

1 cup / 8 fl oz. thick coconut milk (see page 11)

¼ cup / 2 fl oz. avocado oil

1 tsp. guar gum

Walnut Cookies (recipe page 97) – this needs to be made in advance

Warm the cream, almond milk, xylitol, banana and caramel extracts, and sea salt in a medium pan until it just starts to boil. Simmer for 1 minute and then remove from the heat.

Place the thick coconut milk and avocado oil in a blender with the warm banana cream, and blend for 30 seconds.

Turn the blender to low speed, and while the blender is running, add the guar gum by tapping it through the opening in the lid, and blend for 30 seconds.

Pour the ice cream custard into a bowl or jar, cover, and place in the 'fridge for at least 8 hours, but preferably overnight. Don't skip the chillin', no matter which type of churner you have.

Stir the chilled custard well to make sure it is completely mixed and read the churning and freezing section on page 23. Freeze the custard in your churner according to the manufacturer's instructions. It typically takes between 15 - 20 minutes to freeze to a soft-serve consistency.

Once the ice cream has frozen to a soft-serve consistency in the churner, quickly spoon a layer into the bottom of your cold storage container. Sprinkle chilled broken Walnut Cookies over the ice cream. Continue to layer ice cream and cookies until the ice cream has all been removed from the churner.

Cover and place in the freezer for at least 8 hours, preferably overnight.

~~~~~~

I've eaten Banana Cream Pie once in my life: August 3rd, 1993. I remember vividly because I was visiting my friend, Shawn, in Arizona, during my first ever trip to America. I asked what Banana Cream Pie was and his sister rustled one right up for me. It was delicious! An all-American mainstay us Brits never knew about. Here's an ice cream version to celebrate its awesomeness.

Boom! Boom! Basil Ice Cream

1 cup / 8 fl oz. heavy cream (see page 12)

¾ cup / 6 fl oz. almond milk, unsweetened vanilla

4 oz. / 100g xylitol (NO substitutes!)

¾ tsp. sea salt

2 oz. / 55g fresh basil leaves

½ cup / 4 fl oz. thick coconut milk (see page 11)

8 oz. / 225g ricotta cheese

1 TBSP lemon juice

1 tsp. guar gum

Warm the cream, almond milk, xylitol, sea salt, and basil leaves in a medium pan until it just starts to boil. Remove from the heat, cover and leave for an hour to steep.

Pour the basil-infused milk through a sieve to remove the leaves. Press down hard on the leaves to extract as much flavor as possible. DO NOT DISCARD THE LEAVES.

Place the thick coconut milk, ricotta, and lemon juice in a blender with the strained basil-infused milk, and blend on low for 30 seconds. Add 1 packed TBSP of the soggy basil leaves from earlier and blend until the custard is flecked with little basil pieces. So pretty!

With the blender still on low speed, and while the blender is running, add the guar gum by tapping it through the opening in the lid, and blend for 30 seconds.

Pour the ice cream custard into a bowl or jar, cover, and place in the 'fridge for at least 8 hours, but preferably overnight. Don't skip the chillin', no matter which type of churner you have.

Stir the chilled custard well to make sure it is completely mixed and read the churning and freezing section on page 23. Freeze the custard in your churner according to the manufacturer's instructions. It typically takes between 15 - 20 minutes to freeze to a soft-serve consistency.

Once the ice cream has frozen to a soft-serve consistency, quickly transfer it from the churning bowl into your pre-chilled container, and place in the freezer for at least 8 hours, preferably overnight.

~~~~~~

THIS. This Basil Ice Cream is fantastic! Named after the catchphrase of one of my favorite childhood characters – Basil Brush – this ice cream is light, refreshing, intensely basil, and entirely delicious. Boom boom!

PB & C Ice Cream

1 ½ cups / 12 fl oz. hemp milk, unsweetened (see page 12)

½ cup / 4 fl oz. heavy cream (see page 12)

4 ½ oz. / 125g xylitol (NO substitutes!)

½ tsp. sea salt

1 ¼ oz. / 35g raw, unsweetened cocoa powder

1 ½ cups / 12 fl oz. thick coconut milk (see page 11)

1 tsp. vanilla extract

1 tsp. guar gum

Peanut Butter Drops (recipe page 91) – this needs to be made in advance

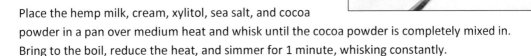

Place the hemp milk, cream, xylitol, sea salt, and cocoa powder in a pan over medium heat and whisk until the cocoa powder is completely mixed in. Bring to the boil, reduce the heat, and simmer for 1 minute, whisking constantly.

Leave to cool stirring well occasionally.

Place the thick coconut milk and vanilla extract in the blender, add the cooled chocolate custard and blend for 10 seconds.

Turn the blender to low speed, and while the blender is running, add the guar gum by tapping it through the opening in the lid, and blend for 30 seconds.

Pour the ice cream custard into a bowl or jar, cover, and place in the 'fridge for at least 8 hours, but preferably overnight. Don't skip the chillin', no matter which type of churner you have.

Stir the chilled custard well to make sure it is completely mixed and read the churning and freezing section on page 23. Freeze the custard in your churner according to the manufacturer's instructions. It typically takes between 15 - 20 minutes to freeze to a soft-serve consistency.

Once the ice cream has frozen to a soft-serve consistency in the churner, quickly spoon a layer of ice cream into the bottom of your cold storage container. Sprinkle Peanut Butter Drops over the ice cream, and then continue to layer ice cream and Peanut Butter Drops until the ice cream has all been removed from the churner.

Cover and place in the freezer for at least 8 hours, preferably overnight.

~~~~~~

Peanut Butter is awesome (if you can tolerate it). That's all I have to say on the matter, but Danny Vega – The Ketogenic Athlete – would heartily agree.

Wondering why the various images of chocolate ice cream all look a little different in color from each other, and may look different to other chocolate ice creams you've eaten?

Here's why:

- Different brands of cocoa powders and chocolates are different colors. I use Valrhona cocoa powder which has a lovely red tint to it.

- The recipes are different. One has 100% chocolate in it as well as cocoa powder, which makes the ice cream darker. I lightened the base chocolate recipes for the Rocky Road and PB & C to allow the flavor of the mix-ins to shine through more, instead of them competing with an intense chocolate flavor. You could use the Kept In The Dark Chocolate base with the mix-ins if you prefer.

- The images were all shot at different times, and light changes everything, including how we perceive colors. An overcast day vs. a bright sunny day can make colors look significantly different.

Talking of chocolate, I spent a couple of years of my life working as a Chocolatier – long before I wised up to the whole sugar-is-making-you-sick thing. I would spend days up to my elbows in thick, dark, molten chocolate while making handmade chocolates in Perth, Australia, and later in London. I also spent time as a Chocolate Sales Rep – extoling the virtues of Valrhona to all the top chefs and retail stores far and wide across England. It was all chocolate, all the time back then; including as much great chocolate as I could eat. Ah, that was the life. Eating chocolate, talking about chocolate, smiling a lot, and getting paid for it.

If you're a lover of this studly bean, you'll be stoked to know that cocoa is all sorts of good for you, just as long as it comes without the sugar. I won't bore you with all the technical geekery, but just know that it is a fabulous source of healthy fats, as well as containing fiber, protein, and bucket loads of minerals and vitamins. Plus, as every woman who has reached child-bearing age knows, chocolate literally makes you happy. Hand over the chocolate and no one gets hurt.

For other delicious recipes using just the cocoa and none of the sugar, head over to www.carriebrown.com, click on the recipes link, and then click on 'Chocolate' in the list of Topics.

All The Beans Ice Cream

1 ¼ cups / 10 fl oz. almond milk, unsweetened vanilla

6 oz. / 170g whole coffee beans

5 oz. / 140g xylitol (NO substitutes!)

1 tsp. sea salt

¾ cup / 6 fl oz. heavy cream (see page 12)

1 ½ cups / 12 fl oz. thick coconut milk (see page 11)

1 tsp. vanilla extract

1 tsp. guar gum

2 oz. / 55g cocoa nibs, chilled in 'fridge

In a pan, bring the almond milk, whole coffee beans, xylitol, sea salt and cream to the boil over a medium heat. Stir. Remove from the heat, cover and leave to steep for an hour.

Strain the coffee-infused milk through a sieve to remove the beans.

Place the thick coconut milk into a blender with the coffee-infused milk, and the vanilla extract, and blend for 10 seconds.

Turn the blender to low speed, and while the blender is running, add the guar gum by tapping it through the opening in the lid, and blend for 30 seconds.

Pour the ice cream custard into a bowl or jar, cover, and place in the 'fridge for at least 8 hours, but preferably overnight. Don't skip the chillin', no matter which type of churner you have.

Stir the chilled custard well to make sure it is completely mixed and read the churning and freezing section on page 23. Freeze the custard in your churner according to the manufacturer's instructions. It typically takes between 15 - 30 minutes to freeze to a soft-serve consistency.

Once the ice cream has frozen to a soft-serve consistency in the churner, pour the chilled cocoa nibs through the opening in the top of the churner and churn until mixed through.

Quickly transfer it from the churning bowl into your pre-chilled container, and place in the freezer for at least 8 hours, preferably overnight.

Note: because of the extra sweetener required for this flavor, the ice cream does not freeze as hard as most. If you can store it in a deep freezer instead of your 'fridge / freezer, I would recommend that you do so. Be very fast when taking it out of the freezer to serve.

Rocky Road Ice Cream

1 ½ cups / 12 fl oz. hemp milk, unsweetened (see page 12)

1 cup / 8 fl oz. heavy cream (see page 12)

4 ½ oz. / 125g xylitol (NO substitutes!)

½ tsp. sea salt

1 ¼ oz. / 35g raw, unsweetened cocoa powder

1 cup / 8 fl oz. thick coconut milk (see page 11)

1 tsp. vanilla extract

1 tsp. guar gum

3 oz. / 85g walnuts, toasted, chopped, and frozen

Sugar-free Marshmallows (recipe page 94) – these need to be made in advance

Place the hemp milk, cream, xylitol, sea salt, and cocoa powder in a pan over medium heat and whisk until the cocoa powder is completely mixed in. Bring to the boil, reduce the heat, and simmer for 1 minute, whisking constantly.

Leave to cool stirring well occasionally.

Place the thick coconut milk and vanilla extract in the blender, add the cooled chocolate custard and blend for 10 seconds.

Turn the blender to low speed, and while the blender is running, add the guar gum by tapping it through the opening in the lid, and blend for 30 seconds.

Pour the ice cream custard into a bowl or jar, cover, and place in the 'fridge for at least 8 hours, but preferably overnight. Don't skip the chillin', no matter which type of churner you have.

Stir the chilled custard well to make sure it is completely mixed and read the churning and freezing section on page 23. Freeze the custard in your churner according to the manufacturer's instructions. It typically takes between 15 - 20 minutes to freeze to a soft-serve consistency.

Once the ice cream has frozen to a soft-serve consistency in the churner, quickly spoon a layer of ice cream into the bottom of your cold storage container. Sprinkle the frozen toasted walnuts and marshmallows over the ice cream, and then continue to layer ice cream, walnuts, and marshmallows until the ice cream has all been removed from the churner.

Cover and place in the freezer for at least 8 hours, preferably overnight.

You're Bacon Me Crazy Ice Cream

1 cup / 8 fl oz. heavy cream (see page 12)

1 ¼ cups / 10 fl oz. hemp milk, unsweetened (see page 12)

4 oz. / 110g xylitol (NO substitutes!)

2 ½ TBSP caramel extract

1 tsp. sea salt

½ cup / 4 fl oz. thick coconut milk (see page 11)

¼ cup / 2 fl oz. avocado oil

2 oz. / 55g full fat cream cheese

1 tsp. guar gum

8 oz. / 225g bacon, cooked (but NOT hard and crispy), chopped into small pieces and chilled

Warm the cream, hemp milk, xylitol, caramel extract, and sea salt in a medium pan until it just starts to boil. Simmer for 1 minute and then remove from the heat.

Place the thick coconut milk, avocado oil, and cream cheese in a blender with the warm caramel cream, and blend on low for 30 seconds.

With the blender on low speed, and while the blender is running, add the guar gum by tapping it through the opening in the lid, and blend for 30 seconds.

Pour the ice cream custard into a bowl or jar, cover, and place in the 'fridge for at least 8 hours, but preferably overnight. Don't skip the chillin', no matter which type of churner you have.

Stir the chilled custard well to make sure it is completely mixed and read the churning and freezing section on page 23. Freeze the custard in your churner according to the manufacturer's instructions. It typically takes between 15 - 20 minutes to freeze to a soft-serve consistency.

Once the ice cream has frozen to a soft-serve consistency, quickly transfer it from the churning bowl into your pre-chilled container and stir in the chopped bacon thoroughly. Be quick so the ice cream doesn't start to melt. Cover and place in the freezer for at least 8 hours, preferably overnight.

~~~~~~

There's something magical about sea salt and caramel together. It is probably my favorite flavor combination – if I had to choose just one. Pre-KETO my favorite chocolates were Fran's Grey Sea Salt Caramels. Well, they still are – I just don't eat them anymore.

While I had never planned to add bacon to my Salty Caramel Ice Cream, the number of requests I had to do so were so loud and numerous I was compelled to oblige. You're bacon me crazy!

Coffee Almond Fudge Ice Cream

1 ¼ cup / 10 fl oz. hemp milk, unsweetened (see page 12)

3 ½ oz. / 100g whole coffee beans

4 ½ oz. / 125g xylitol (NO substitutes!)

1 tsp. sea salt

1 ½ cups / 12 fl oz. heavy cream (see page 12)

¾ cup / 6 fl oz. thick coconut milk (see page 11)

1 tsp. vanilla extract

1 tsp. guar gum

4 oz. / 110g slivered almonds, toasted, and frozen

½ batch Chocolate Fudge Ripple (recipe page 87) – this needs to be made in advance

In a pan, bring the hemp milk, whole coffee beans, xylitol, sea salt, and ½ cup of the cream to the boil over a medium heat. Stir. Remove from the heat, cover and leave to steep for an hour.

Strain the coffee-infused milk through a sieve to remove the beans. (Dry the beans overnight, grind them finely, and then use them to fertilize your roses. BEST. ROSES. EVER.)

Place the thick coconut milk, the remaining 1 cup of cream, coffee-infused milk, and the vanilla extract into a blender. Blend for 10 seconds.

Turn the blender to low speed, and while the blender is running, add the guar gum by tapping it through the opening in the lid, and blend for 30 seconds.

Pour the ice cream custard into a bowl or jar, cover, and place in the 'fridge for at least 8 hours, but preferably overnight. Don't skip the chillin', no matter which type of churner you have.

Stir the chilled custard well to make sure it is completely mixed and read the churning and freezing section on page 23. Freeze the custard in your churner according to the manufacturer's instructions. It typically takes between 15 - 20 minutes to freeze to a soft-serve consistency.

Once the ice cream has frozen to a soft-serve consistency in the churner, add the toasted frozen almonds to the churner through the opening in the top, and churn until mixed through.

Quickly spoon a layer of ice cream into the bottom of your cold storage container. Spoon large dollops of Chocolate Fudge Ripple over the ice cream, and then continue to layer ice cream and fudge until the ice cream has all been removed from the churner. Be careful to 'dollop' the ice cream layer over the Fudge Ripple so that there is as little movement of the fudge as possible. Otherwise you will get 'muddy' ice cream.

Cover and place in the freezer for at least 8 hours, preferably overnight.

Rascally Raspberry Ice Cream

12 oz. / 500g fresh or frozen raspberries

1 cup / 8 fl oz. thick coconut milk (see page 11)

½ cup / 4 fl oz. almond milk, unsweetened vanilla

1 cup / 8 fl oz. heavy cream (see page 12)

3 ½ oz. / 100g xylitol (NO substitutes!)

½ tsp. sea salt

1 ½ TBSP lemon juice

1 tsp. guar gum

Heat raspberries in a pan over a medium heat until they are very soft – about 15 minutes.

Press the raspberry pulp through a sieve to remove all the seeds. This will take a little while, but will be SO worth the effort! DO NOT puree the raspberries before you sieve them to save you a few minutes. You will end up with a "dusty" taste in the final ice cream. True story.

Place the raspberry puree, thick coconut milk, almond milk, cream, xylitol, sea salt, and lemon juice into a blender and blend for 10 seconds.

Turn the blender to low speed, and while the blender is running, add the guar gum by tapping it through the opening in the lid, and blend for 30 seconds.

Pour the ice cream custard into a bowl or jar, cover, and place in the 'fridge for at least 8 hours, but preferably overnight. Don't skip the chillin', no matter which type of churner you have.

Stir the chilled custard well to make sure it is completely mixed and read the churning and freezing section on page 23. Freeze the custard in your churner according to the manufacturer's instructions. It typically takes between 15 - 20 minutes to freeze to a soft-serve consistency.

Once the ice cream has frozen to a soft-serve consistency, quickly transfer it from the churning bowl into your pre-chilled container, and place in the freezer for at least 8 hours, preferably overnight.

~~~~~~

In honor of the first ice cream I ever made, this was a no-brainer flavor for a spot in this book. I still remember the sheer delight of dishing up that first scoop of raspberry scrumptiousness, and feeling like a 3-year-old jumping in mud puddles as the "Yums!" ran around the table.

If you like raspberries, you're gonna adore this ice cream.

Blueberry Cheesecake Ice Cream

8 oz. / 225g full fat cream cheese

Zest of 1 lemon

1 cup / 8 fl oz. sour cream

1 tsp. sea salt

4 ½ oz. / 125g xylitol (NO substitutes!)

1 cup / 8 fl oz. almond milk, unsweetened vanilla

½ cup / 4 fl oz. heavy cream (see page 12)

½ tsp. lemon extract

Blueberry Compote (recipe page 85), chilled – this needs to be made in advance

Place the cream cheese, lemon zest, sour cream, sea salt, xylitol, almond milk, cream, and lemon extract into a food processor and blend for 30 seconds.

Pour the ice cream custard into a bowl or jar, cover, and place in the 'fridge for at least 8 hours, but preferably overnight. Don't skip the chillin', no matter which type of churner you have.

Stir the chilled custard well to make sure it is completely mixed and read the churning and freezing section on page 23. Freeze the custard in your churner according to the manufacturer's instructions. It typically takes between 15 - 20 minutes to freeze to a soft-serve consistency.

Once the ice cream has frozen to a soft-serve consistency, quickly spoon a layer of ice cream into the bottom of your cold storage container. Spoon dollops of chilled Blueberry Sauce over the ice cream, and then continue to layer ice cream and blueberry sauce until the ice cream has all been removed from the churner. Be careful to dollop the ice cream and not stir. You don't want "muddy" ice cream.

Cover and place in the freezer for at least 8 hours, preferably overnight.

~~~~~~

Forrest: holy $#@% that's good.

Forrest: Seriously. Eric and I are supposed to be discussing sales quotas…and we're just staring at each other.

CB: :-)

Forrest: Yes – like that. :->> more like that. All hopped up on delicious.

Wimbledon Strawberry Ice Cream

½ cup / 4 fl oz. almond milk, unsweetened vanilla

½ cup / 4 fl oz. heavy cream (see page 12)

½ cup / 4 fl oz. thick coconut milk (see page 11)

1 ¾ oz. / 50g xylitol (NO substitutes!)

½ tsp. sea salt

¼ tsp. vanilla extract

½ tsp. guar gum

6 oz. / 170g fresh strawberries, roughly chopped into small pieces (if you leave them large they will freeze too hard)

1 oz. / 30g xylitol

Place the almond milk, cream, thick coconut milk, xylitol, sea salt, and vanilla in a blender and blend for 10 seconds.

Turn the blender to low speed, and while the blender is running, add the guar gum by tapping it through the opening in the lid, and blend for 30 seconds.

Pour the ice cream custard into a bowl or jar, cover, and place in the 'fridge for at least 8 hours, but preferably overnight. Don't skip the chillin', no matter which type of churner you have.

Meanwhile, place the chopped strawberries in a bowl with 1 oz. / 30g xylitol and mix well. Cover and leave to marinate in the 'fridge while the ice cream chills, stirring often. The strawberries will become very juicy. Yum.

Stir the chilled custard well to make sure it is completely mixed and read the churning and freezing section on page 23. Freeze the custard in your churner according to the manufacturer's instructions. It typically takes between 15 - 20 minutes to freeze to a soft-serve consistency.

Once the ice cream has frozen to a soft-serve consistency in the churner, add the chilled marinated strawberry pieces to the churner and churn until mixed through.

Quickly transfer it from the churning bowl into your pre-chilled container, and place in the freezer for at least 8 hours, preferably overnight.

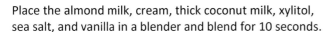

This ice cream reminds me of summers in England: Wimbledon, the end of exams, warm, gentle breezes, picnics on the lawn, sunshine, meandering down the banks of the river Thames, roses in full bloom, strolling in Hyde Park, boating in Henley, bowlfuls of fresh strawberries and cream, 7-week-long holidays from school, Mr. Whippy Ice Cream, and Cadbury's flakes. Ah, summer.

Cranberry Schmanberry Ice Cream

10 oz. / 280g cranberries

4 ½ oz. / 125g xylitol (NO substitutes!)

½ cup / 4 fl oz. almond milk, unsweetened vanilla

1½ cups / 12 fl oz. heavy cream (see page 12)

1 tsp. cinnamon extract

2 tsp. orange extract

½ tsp. sea salt

½ cup / 4 fl oz. thick coconut milk (see page 11)

1 tsp. guar gum

Place the cranberries and xylitol in a pan over medium heat and cook for 15 minutes until the cranberries are very soft.

Blend the cooked cranberries until they are very smooth and then press through a fine mesh sieve to remove any remaining seed and skins.

Return the cranberry puree to the pan and add the almond milk, cream, cinnamon and orange extracts, and sea salt. Heat until the mixture just starts to boil. Simmer for 1 minute and then remove from the heat.

Place the thick coconut milk in a blender with the cranberry cream and blend for 10 seconds.

Turn the blender to low speed, and while the blender is running, add the guar gum by tapping it through the opening in the lid, and blend for 30 seconds.

Pour the ice cream custard into a bowl or jar, cover, and place in the 'fridge for at least 8 hours, but preferably overnight. Don't skip the chillin', no matter which type of churner you have.

Stir the chilled custard well to make sure it is completely mixed and read the churning and freezing section on page 23. Freeze the custard in your churner according to the manufacturer's instructions. It typically takes between 15 - 20 minutes to freeze to a soft-serve consistency.

Once the ice cream has frozen to a soft-serve consistency, quickly transfer it from the churning bowl into your pre-chilled container, and place in the freezer for at least 8 hours, preferably overnight.

~~~~~~

Cranberries! That aren't made into Cranberry Sauce and eaten with turkey! YAY!!

Bubblegum Bliss Ice Cream

1 lb. / 450g fresh strawberries, hulled

1 cup / 8 fl oz. almond milk, unsweetened vanilla

3 oz. / 85g xylitol (NO substitutes!)

½ tsp. sea salt

1 cup / 8 fl oz. heavy cream (see page 12)

1 tsp. banana extract

1 tsp. vanilla extract

1 tsp. orange extract

1 tsp. lemon extract

1 cup / 8 fl oz. thick coconut milk (see page 11)

1 tsp. guar gum

Marshmallows - (recipe page 94) – this needs to be made in advance

Strawberry Ripple - (recipe page 86) – this needs to be made in advance of churning

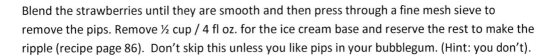

Blend the strawberries until they are smooth and then press through a fine mesh sieve to remove the pips. Remove ½ cup / 4 fl oz. for the ice cream base and reserve the rest to make the ripple (recipe page 86). Don't skip this unless you like pips in your bubblegum. (Hint: you don't).

Warm the almond milk, xylitol, sea salt, cream, and all 4 extracts in a medium pan until it just starts to boil. Simmer for one minute and then remove from the heat.

Place the thick coconut milk in a blender with the bubblegum cream and blend for 10 seconds. Add ½ cup / 4 fl oz. of the strawberry puree that you made earlier.

Turn the blender to low speed, and while the blender is running, add the guar gum by tapping it through the opening in the lid, and blend for 30 seconds.

Pour the ice cream custard into a bowl or jar, cover, and place in the 'fridge for at least 8 hours, but preferably overnight. Don't skip the chillin', no matter which type of churner you have.

Stir the chilled custard well to make sure it is completely mixed and read the churning and freezing section on page 23. Freeze the custard in your churner according to the manufacturer's instructions. It typically takes between 15 – 20 minutes to freeze to a soft-serve consistency.

Once the ice cream has frozen to a soft-serve consistency, quickly spoon a layer of ice cream into the bottom of your cold storage container. Sprinkle liberally with marshmallows and then spoon dollops of chilled Strawberry Ripple over the ice cream. Continue to layer ice cream, marshmallows and Strawberry Ripple until the ice cream has all been removed from the churner. Be careful to dollop the ice cream and not stir. You don't want "muddy" ice cream.

Mind Blowing Blackberry Ice Cream

20 oz. / 560g fresh blackberries

2 TBSP water

3 ½ oz. / 100g xylitol (NO substitutes!)

½ tsp. sea salt

2 tsp. lemon juice

1 TBSP kirsch (cherry liqueur)

½ cup / 4 fl oz. heavy cream (see page 12)

½ cup / 4 fl oz. thick coconut milk (see page 11)

7 ½ oz. / 210g crème fraiche

½ tsp. guar gum

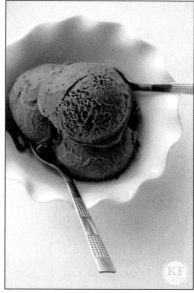

Place blackberries and water in a pan over medium heat and cook, stirring occasionally, until the berries are very soft – about 10 minutes.

Carefully pour the cooked berries into a blender and blend on high until the fruit is pureed. Rinse out the pan you used, place a sieve on it, and press the puree through the sieve. Use a clean spatula to scrape the puree from the underside of the sieve when finished.

Put the pan back over medium heat, add the xylitol, sea salt, lemon juice, kirsch, and cream. Stir well and bring just to a boil. Reduce heat and simmer for 1 minute. Remove and let cool for 10 minutes before carefully pouring the warm puree into a clean blender. Add the thick coconut milk and crème fraiche and blend for 10 seconds.

Turn the blender to low speed, and while the blender is running, add the guar gum by tapping it through the opening in the lid, and blend for 30 seconds.

Pour the ice cream custard into a bowl or jar, cover, and place in the 'fridge for at least 8 hours, but preferably overnight. Don't skip the chillin', no matter which type of churner you have.

Stir the chilled custard well to make sure it is completely mixed and read the churning and freezing section on page 23. Freeze the custard in your churner according to the manufacturer's instructions. It typically takes between 20 – 30 minutes to freeze to a soft-serve consistency.

Once the ice cream has frozen to a soft-serve consistency, quickly transfer it from the churning bowl into your pre-chilled container, and place in the freezer for at least 8 hours, preferably overnight.

~~~~~~

Heavens to Betsy. The texture! The flavor! Prepare to have your mind blown by blackberries!

Strawberry Rhubarb Pie Ice Cream

14 oz. / 390g rhubarb, trimmed and roughly chopped

7 oz. / 195g strawberries, roughly chopped

5 ½ oz. / 155g xylitol (NO substitutes!)

2 ½ TBSP kirsch (cherry liqueur)

½ cup / 4 fl oz. almond milk, unsweetened vanilla

1 cup / 8 fl oz. heavy cream (see page 12)

¾ cup / 6 fl oz. thick coconut milk (see page 11)

½ tsp. sea salt

1 tsp. guar gum

Cinnamon Shortbread Cookies (recipe page 96) – this needs to be made in advance

Place the rhubarb, strawberries, xylitol and kirsch in a pan and simmer for 15 minutes until the fruit is completely soft. Remove from the heat and let cool for 15 minutes.

Place the almond milk, cream, thick coconut milk and sea salt in a blender with the warm fruit compote, and blend until completely smooth.

Turn the blender to low speed, and while the blender is running, add the guar gum by tapping it through the opening in the lid, and blend for 30 seconds.

Pour the ice cream custard into a bowl or jar, cover, and place in the 'fridge for at least 8 hours, but preferably overnight. Don't skip the chillin', no matter which type of churner you have.

Stir the chilled custard well to make sure it is completely mixed and read the churning and freezing section on page 23. Freeze the custard in your churner according to the manufacturer's instructions. It typically takes between 15 - 20 minutes to freeze to a soft-serve consistency.

Once the ice cream has frozen to a soft-serve consistency in the churner, quickly spoon a layer into the bottom of your cold storage container. Sprinkle chilled broken Cinnamon Shortbread Cookies over the ice cream. Continue to layer ice cream and cookies until the ice cream has all been removed from the churner.

Cover and place in the freezer for at least 8 hours, preferably overnight.

~~~~~~

Strawberry Rhubarb Pie is another all-American *thing* that had never made it to my "must eat" list. They weren't something I grew up with, so it had never occurred to me that it was such a magical combination. So, I literally swooned over the blender when I had the first taste of the custard and am now a bona fide Strawberry Rhubarb fan.

Double Cherry Choc Chunk Ice Cream

1 ¼ cups / 10 fl oz. almond milk, unsweetened vanilla

3 oz. / 85g xylitol (NO substitutes!)

4 TBSP cherry extract

1 cup / 8 fl oz. heavy cream (see page 12)

½ tsp. sea salt

7 ½ oz. / 210g crème fraiche

¼ cup / 2 fl oz. avocado oil

1 tsp. guar gum

Chocolate Chunks (recipe page 93) – this needs to be made in advance

Sour Cherry Chunks (recipe page 89) – this needs to be made in advance

Warm the almond milk, xylitol, cherry extract, cream, and sea salt in a medium pan until it just starts to boil. Simmer for 1 minute, then remove from the heat and cool for 15 minutes.

Carefully pour the cherry cream mixture into a blender, add the crème fraiche and avocado oil and blend for 10 seconds.

Turn the blender to low speed, and while the blender is running, add the guar gum by tapping it through the opening in the lid, and blend for 30 seconds.

Pour the ice cream custard into a bowl or jar, cover, and place in the 'fridge for at least 8 hours, but preferably overnight. Don't skip the chillin', no matter which type of churner you have.

When you are ready to churn, place a mixing bowl in the freezer to chill. Stir the chilled custard well to make sure it is completely mixed and read the churning and freezing section on page 23. Freeze the custard in your churner according to the manufacturer's instructions. It typically takes between 20 – 30 minutes to freeze to a soft-serve consistency.

Once the ice cream has frozen to a soft-serve consistency, quickly transfer it from the churning bowl into the pre-chilled mixing bowl. Add the frozen Chocolate Chunks and the Sour Cherry Chunks to the bowl and mix into the ice cream as quickly as you can. Turn into a container, cover, and place in the freezer for at least 8 hours, preferably overnight.

~~~~~~

THIS IS IT, PEOPLE.

The #1 requested ice cream, and the #1 best seller for Ben and Jerry.

I give you a KETO version of Ben & Jerry's Cherry Garcia™ . Our lives are now complete.

Amaretto Cherry Ripple Ice Cream

1 ¼ cup / 10 fl oz. heavy cream (see page 12)

1 ¼ cup / 10 fl oz. almond milk

4 ½ oz. / 125g xylitol (NO substitutes!)

1 tsp. sea salt

½ tsp. amaretto extract

1 tsp. almond extract

½ cup / 4 fl oz. thick coconut milk (see page 11)

¼ cup / 2 fl oz. avocado oil

2 oz. / 55g cream cheese (full fat)

½ tsp. guar gum

Sour Cherry Ripple (recipe page 86) – this needs to be made in advance of churning

Warm the cream, almond milk, xylitol, sea salt, amaretto and almond extracts in a medium pan until it just starts to boil. Simmer for 1 minute, then remove from the heat. Cool slightly.

Carefully pour the cream mixture into a blender, add the thick coconut milk, avocado oil, and cream cheese and blend until cream cheese is completely combined and smooth.

Turn the blender to low speed, and while the blender is running, add the guar gum by tapping it through the opening in the lid, and blend for 30 seconds.

Pour the ice cream custard into a bowl or jar, cover, and place in the 'fridge for at least 8 hours, but preferably overnight. Don't skip the chillin', no matter which type of churner you have.

Stir the chilled custard well to make sure it is completely mixed and read the churning and freezing section on page 23. Freeze the custard in your churner according to the manufacturer's instructions. It typically takes between 15 - 20 minutes to freeze to a soft-serve consistency.

Once the ice cream has frozen to a soft-serve consistency, quickly spoon a layer of ice cream into the bottom of your cold storage container. Spoon dollops of chilled Sour Cherry Ripple over the ice cream, and then continue to layer ice cream and Sour Cherry Ripple until the ice cream has all been removed from the churner. Be careful to dollop the ice cream and not stir. You don't want "muddy" ice cream.

Cover and place in the freezer for at least 8 hours, preferably overnight.

~~~~~~

Black Cherry Amaretto is my all-time fave flavor combo. Given black (and regular) cherries have too much sugar onboard, I had to replicate this using unsweetened sour cherries. Here it is.

White Christmas Ice Cream

8 oz. / 225g cranberries

5 oz. / 110g xylitol (NO substitutes!)

1 cup / 8 fl oz. heavy cream (see page 12)

½ cup / 4 fl oz. almond milk, unsweetened vanilla

½ tsp. sea salt

2 tsp. vanilla extract

4 oz. / 110g food grade cocoa butter

1 cup / 8 fl oz. thick coconut milk (see page 11)

1 tsp. guar gum

Cook the cranberries and xylitol in a pan over medium heat for 15 minutes, stirring gently. Be careful not smash the berries.

Add the cream, almond milk, sea salt, and vanilla extract to the cranberries in the pan and stir gently until combined.

Place a sieve over a clean bowl and pour the cranberries into the sieve. Do not push the cranberries through the sieve but just stir gently and let the liquid fall to the bowl below, leaving the whole cranberries behind. Reserve the cranberries in the fridge for mixing into the churned ice cream.

Return the cream mixture to the pan over a medium heat, and add the chopped cocoa butter, stirring well until it is completely melted. Place the thick coconut milk in a blender with the cocoa butter mixture and blend for 10 seconds.

Turn the blender to low speed, and while the blender is running, add the guar gum by tapping it through the opening in the lid, and blend for 30 seconds.

Pour the ice cream custard into a bowl or jar, cover, and place in the 'fridge for at least 8 hours, but preferably overnight. Don't skip the chillin', no matter which type of churner you have.

Stir the chilled custard well to make sure it is completely mixed and read the churning and freezing section on page 23. Freeze the custard in your churner according to the manufacturer's instructions. It typically takes between 15 - 20 minutes to freeze to a soft-serve consistency.

Once the ice cream has frozen to a soft-serve consistency in the churner, pour the chilled cranberries through the opening in the top of the churner and churn until mixed through.

Quickly transfer it from the churning bowl into your pre-chilled container, cover, and place in the freezer for at least 8 hours, preferably overnight.

Boy Howdy Blueberry Ice Cream

¾ cup / 6 fl oz. almond milk, unsweetened vanilla

3 ½ oz. / 100g xylitol (NO substitutes!)

½ tsp. sea salt

1 ½ tsp. cinnamon extract

¾ cup / 6 fl oz. heavy cream (see page 12)

8 oz. / 225g fresh blueberries

½ cups / 4 fl oz. thick coconut milk (see page 11)

4 oz. / 110g cream cheese

1 tsp. guar gum

Warm the almond milk, xylitol, sea salt, cinnamon extract, and cream in a medium pan until it just starts to boil. Remove from the heat and carefully pour into a blender.

Immediately add the fresh blueberries and blend until smooth.

Add the thick coconut milk and cream cheese to the warm blueberry cream and blend on low until completely smooth.

With the blender still on low speed, and while the blender is running, add the guar gum by tapping it through the opening in the lid, and blend for 30 seconds.

Pour the ice cream custard into a bowl or jar, cover, and place in the 'fridge for at least 8 hours, but preferably overnight. Don't skip the chillin', no matter which type of churner you have.

Stir the chilled custard well to make sure it is completely mixed and read the churning and freezing section on page 23. Freeze the custard in your churner according to the manufacturer's instructions. It typically takes between 15 - 20 minutes to freeze to a soft-serve consistency.

Once the ice cream has frozen to a soft-serve consistency, quickly transfer it from the churning bowl into your pre-chilled container, and place in the freezer for at least 8 hours, preferably overnight.

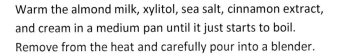

Fantastical purple ice cream!

Confused about the addition of cinnamon? Cinnamon makes the flavor of blueberries pop, so you need less blueberries to get a more intense blueberry flavor. Mother Nature is magical!

Sassy Goat Ice Cream

½ cup / 4 fl oz. almond milk, unsweetened vanilla

4 oz. / 110g xylitol (NO substitutes!)

½ tsp. sea salt

2 cups / 16 fl oz. heavy cream (see page 12)

5 oz. / 140g goat cheese (chevre)

¼ oz. / 7g fresh mint, finely chopped

1 tsp. guar gum

Chunky Strawberry Compote (recipe page 85) – this needs to be made in advance

Place the almond milk, xylitol, sea salt, cream, and goat cheese in a blender and blend on LOW for 5 minutes.

With the blender still on low speed, and while the blender is running, add the finely chopped mint followed by the guar gum by tapping them through the opening in the lid, and blend for 30 seconds.

Pour the ice cream custard into a bowl or jar, cover, and place in the 'fridge for at least 8 hours, but preferably overnight. Don't skip the chillin', no matter which type of churner you have.

Stir the chilled custard well to make sure it is completely mixed and read the churning and freezing section on page 23. Freeze the custard in your churner according to the manufacturer's instructions. It typically takes between 15 - 20 minutes to freeze to a soft-serve consistency.

Once the ice cream has frozen to a soft-serve consistency, quickly spoon a layer of ice cream into the bottom of your cold storage container. Spoon dollops of chilled Chunky Strawberry Compote over the ice cream, and then continue to layer ice cream and Compote until the ice cream has all been removed from the churner. Be careful to dollop the ice cream and not stir. You don't want "muddy" ice cream.

Cover and place in the freezer for at least 8 hours, preferably overnight.

~~~~~~

Goats Cheese Ice Cream studded with fresh mint and rippled with Chunky Strawberry Compote.

Oh. My. Word.

This was consistently in every Taste Testers Top 3. The texture is incredibly smooth and dense, and the fresh mint makes it come alive. The Chunky Strawberry Compote takes it to a whole other level, but if you want to make it super-KETO or you can't do any fruits, omit the compote. The Goats Cheese Ice Cream studded with fresh mint alone is spectacular.

Please try it. Even if it sounds weird.

Apricot Cardamom Ice Cream (Low Carb)

8 oz. / 225g fresh apricots, stoned

1 cup / 8 fl oz. almond milk, unsweetened vanilla

½ cup / 4 fl oz. heavy (double) cream

3 ½ oz. / 100g xylitol (NO substitutes!)

½ tsp. sea salt

1 cup / 8 fl oz. thick coconut milk

¾ tsp. ground cardamom

1 tsp. guar gum

8 oz. / 225g fresh apricots, stoned and chopped into small pieces

1 oz. / 30g xylitol

Simmer 8 oz. / 225g apricots, almond milk, cream, 3 ½ oz. / 100g xylitol and salt over medium heat until apricots are very soft.

Blend the apricot mixture on high until completely smooth and then press through a fine mesh sieve.

Place the thick coconut milk and ground cardamom in the blender, add the apricot puree and blend for 10 seconds.

Turn the blender to low speed, and while the blender is running, add the guar gum by tapping it through the opening in the lid, and blend for 30 seconds.

Pour the ice cream custard into a bowl or jar, cover, and place in the 'fridge for at least 8 hours, but preferably overnight. Don't skip the chillin', no matter which type of churner you have.

At least an hour before churning, mix the remaining 8 oz. / 225g chopped apricots in a bowl with 1 oz. / 30g xylitol and stir well. Leave to marinate, stirring often.

Stir the chilled custard well to make sure it is completely mixed and read the churning and freezing section on page 23. Freeze the custard in your churner according to the manufacturer's instructions. It typically takes between 15 - 20 minutes to freeze to a soft-serve consistency.

Once the ice cream has frozen to a soft-serve consistency, carefully pour the chopped apricots into the churner and continue churning until mixed through.

Quickly transfer it from the churning bowl into your pre-chilled container, cover, and place in the freezer for at least 8 hours, preferably overnight.

Apple Pie a la Mode Ice Cream (Low Carb)

1 ¼ cup / 10 fl oz. heavy cream (see page 12)

1 ½ cup / 12 fl oz. hemp milk, unsweetened (see page 12)

3 ½ oz. / 100g xylitol (NO substitutes!)

1 tsp. sea salt

1 cup / 8 fl oz. thick coconut milk (see page 11)

¼ cup / 2 fl oz. avocado oil

2 tsp. vanilla extract

1 tsp. guar gum

Apple Ripple (recipe page 89) – this needs to be made in advance

Shortbread (recipe page 96) – this needs to be made in advance

Place cream, hemp milk, xylitol, and sea salt in a pan and heat until it just starts to boil. Remove from the heat and allow to cool for 15 minutes.

Place the cooled cream, thick coconut milk, avocado oil, and vanilla extract in the blender and blend for 10 seconds.

Turn the blender to low speed, and while the blender is running, add the guar gum by tapping them through the opening in the lid, and blend for 30 seconds.

Pour the ice cream custard into a bowl or jar, cover, and place in the 'fridge for at least 8 hours, but preferably overnight. Don't skip the chillin', no matter which type of churner you have.

Stir the chilled custard well to make sure it is completely mixed and read the churning and freezing section on page 23. Freeze the custard in your churner according to the manufacturer's instructions. It typically takes between 15 – 20 minutes to freeze to a soft-serve consistency.

Once the ice cream has frozen to a soft-serve consistency in the churner, quickly spoon a layer into the bottom of your cold storage container. Sprinkle chilled broken Lemon Shortbread Cookies over the ice cream and then spoonsful of Apple Ripple. Continue to layer ice cream, cookies, and Apple Ripple until the ice cream has all been removed from the churner.

Cover and place in the freezer for at least 8 hours, preferably overnight.

~~~~~~

Why are there 3 low carb ice creams in a KETO Ice Cream Cookbook? Because some people are less insulin-resistant and / or are further along in their journey and they can eat small amounts of higher-carb fruits without compromising their health or progress. If that's not you, skip these 3 for now.

Peaches and Cream Ice Cream (Low Carb)

½ cup / 4 fl oz. hemp milk, unsweetened (see page 12)

10 oz. / 280g fresh peaches, stones removed

1 cup / 8 fl oz. heavy (double) cream

¾ tsp. sea salt

3 ½ oz. / 100g xylitol (NO substitutes!)

1 cup / 8 fl oz. thick coconut milk

1 tsp. guar gum

7 oz. / 200g fresh peaches, stones removed and chopped into small pieces

1 oz. / 30g xylitol

Place hemp milk, 10oz / 280g peaches, cream, sea salt, and 3 ½ oz. / 100g xylitol in a pan and simmer over a medium heat until peaches are very soft – about 15 minutes.

Place the peach mixture in a blender and blend until completely smooth.

Pass through a fine sieve to remove any peach fibers.

Place the peach puree and thick coconut milk in the blender and blend for 10 seconds.

Turn the blender to low speed, and while the blender is running, add the guar gum by tapping it through the opening in the lid, and blend for 30 seconds.

Pour the ice cream custard into a bowl or jar, cover, and place in the 'fridge for at least 8 hours, but preferably overnight. Don't skip the chillin', no matter which type of churner you have.

Meanwhile, place the remaining 7 oz. / 200g chopped peaches in a bowl with 1 oz. / 30g xylitol and mix well. Cover and leave to marinate for at least an hour, stirring often.

Stir the chilled custard well to make sure it is completely mixed and read the churning and freezing section on page 23. Freeze the custard in your churner according to the manufacturer's instructions. It typically takes between 15 - 20 minutes to freeze to a soft-serve consistency.

Once the ice cream has frozen to a soft-serve consistency in the churner, add the marinated peach pieces to the churner and churn until mixed through.

Quickly transfer it from the churning bowl into your pre-chilled container, cover, and place in the freezer for at least 8 hours, preferably overnight.

Chunky Compotes – Blueberry / Strawberry

10 oz. / 280g fresh blueberries **OR** fresh strawberries

1 ¾ oz. / 50g xylitol (NO substitutes!)

1 TBSP water

1 TBSP lemon juice

½ tsp. guar gum

2 tsp. kirsch (cherry liqueur)

{If making Chunky Strawberry Compote, hull and roughly chop the strawberries into a size you wouldn't mind biting into with your ice cream}.

Put the berries and xylitol in a small pan, stir well, and heat until the berries become juicy and start to breakdown. Add the water and lemon juice and stir well.

Sprinkle the guar gum gently and evenly over the surface of the berries and juices, and mix very rapidly to disperse the gum evenly throughout. Continue to stir over the heat until the mixture has thickened.

Remove from the heat, add the kirsch and stir well. Leave to cool before placing in an air-tight container in the 'fridge until use. Use well chilled.

~~~~~~

The first time I ever ate a blueberry I was living in Canada, way up in the Rocky Mountains, 3 hours west of Banff. That was also the first time I ate nachos, bought soft-serve in a waxed carton to take home, saw a 15" pizza, and roasted marshmallows over a camp fire; not to mention it was the first time I gobbled up thick American pancakes, and ate bacon with maple syrup all over it. Who knew I would encounter so many culinary firsts up in the Great White North? Fun times!

I hold a lot of fondness for Canada. There were so many firsts – I waterskied, rode horses, drove a truck, and went to a rodeo – The Calgary Stampede no less! – saw bears in the wild, went to the World's Fair in Vancouver, wore shorts for 3 months straight, and fell in love with a particularly rugged and handsome Oil Driller called Kevin. We met over a garbage can at the Expo, but that's a whole other story that it's probably best I don't get into.

I'm not one for eating blueberries straight – in the raw so to speak – but make a sauce and layer it with cheesecake ice cream? Or make a green smoothie and toss some in? How about Lemon Blueberry Scones? YES, please!

There's the Boy Howdy Blueberry Ice Cream on page 79 which is all blueberries all the time.

There's also blueberries galore over at www.carriebrown.com and click on the recipes link.

Strawberry Ripple

Remaining Strawberry Puree from Bubblegum Bliss Ice Cream – recipe page 73

3 oz. / 85g xylitol (NO substitutes!)

1 TBSP vegetable glycerin

1 TBSP lemon juice

¾ tsp. guar gum

Put the strawberry puree, xylitol, glycerin, and lemon juice in a small pan over medium heat and bring just to the boil.

Gently and evenly sprinkle the guar gum over the surface while whisk vigorously with the other hand to incorporate the gum into the ripple.

Simmer for a minute until the ripple has thickened. Remove from the heat and allow to cool completely.

Pour into an airtight container and store in the fridge until you are ready to layer it into freshly churned Bubblegum Bliss Ice Cream – page 73.

~~~~~~

Sour Cherry Ripple

15 oz. / 420g sour cherries (canned), **very well drained**

4 oz. / 110g xylitol (NO substitutes!)

2 ¼ TBSP cherry extract

½ tsp. guar gum

Put the drained cherries, xylitol, and cherry extract in a small pan over medium heat and bring just to the boil. Simmer for one minute, remove from the heat and cool for 15 minutes.

Carefully pour the cherry ripple into a blender, and with the blender on low speed, and while the blender is running, add the guar gum by tapping it through the opening in the lid, and blend for 30 seconds.

Pour into an airtight container and store in the fridge until you are ready to layer it into freshly churned Amaretto Cherry Ripple Ice Cream – page 77.

Chocolate Fudge Ripple

1 cup / 8 fl oz. thick coconut milk **OR** heavy cream (see pages 11 and 12)

5 oz. / 140g sugar-free marshmallows (recipe page 94)

1 oz. / 30g cocoa powder, unsweetened

4 oz. / 110g 100% cocoa solids chocolate (unsweetened), chopped

2 TBSP vegetable glycerin

½ tsp. vanilla extract

Warm the thick coconut milk or cream in a pan over medium heat. Add the sugar-free marshmallows to the pan and stir constantly until the marshmallows are completely melted. Sieve the cocoa powder directly into the pan, and whisk well until completely mixed into the marshmallow mixture.

Remove the pan from the heat and add the chopped chocolate. Stir well until the chocolate is completely melted. Add the glycerin and vanilla extract and stir well.

Pour into a glass bowl or dish and leave to cool completely. Once cold, cover and store in the 'fridge.

~~~~~~

This ripple is extremely thick. And dark, and shiny, and chocolaty, and utterly, utterly glorious. It's also quick and easy to sling together once you've got the sugar-free marshmallows made. It is extremely stable and does not freeze any harder than it is when it is completely cooled.

When I created this final version, I was so happy I cried. If only you knew the trials and tribulations that I went through to get you a fantastic KETO Chocolate Fudge Ripple for your ice cream. One that stays soft, and gooey, and luscious at -18C. You're so worth it.

PS. If you make it a while in advance and it goes dull or stiffens, just warm gently and let cool again.

You can also use this as a fantastic sauce for pouring over anything you feel like pouring chocolate fudge sauce over.

It keeps in the fridge for ages – like weeks, so make up a big batch and keep some handy for your emergency Chocolate Fudge Sauce needs.

You'll be using this recipe a lot, I guarantee it.

Bacon Ripple

12 oz. / 335g bacon

3 oz. / 85g xylitol (NO substitutes!)

2 TBSP apple cider vinegar

1 ½ cups / 12 fl oz. water

½ tsp. liquid smoke

1 ½ TBSP maple extract

1 ½ TBSP vegetable glycerin

1 TBSP avocado oil

½ tsp. guar gum

Chop the bacon into small pieces – think how big you want in a bite of ice cream – and sauté over a medium heat in a frying pan until cooked, but not crispy.

Carefully drain off the liquid fat, and then tip the bacon onto several sheets of kitchen paper to absorb any excess grease.

Return the bacon pieces to the pan and add the xylitol, apple cider vinegar, water, liquid smoke, maple extract and vegetable glycerin. Stir well and bring to the boil over a medium heat.

Pour the avocado oil into a small dish and add the guar gum. Stir well until the guar gum is completely mixed in.

Pour the guar mixture into the hot bacon sauce and stir well until the sauce is thickened.

Remove from the heat and allow to cool. Pour into an airtight container and store in the fridge until you want to ripple it into the freshly churned Maple Bacon Crack Ice Cream – page 50.

~~~~~~

I don't even know what to say about this stuff. How about, it's completely awesome. And rippled into KETO Maple Bacon Crack Ice Cream? Ridiculous.

You could also use this in the You're Bacon Me Crazy Ice Cream on page 67 instead of plain chopped bacon, if you have the time and inclination. Whatever floats your boat. Just do you.

Apple Ripple

1 lb. / 450g Granny Smith (or similarly less-sweet) apples

2 oz. / 55g xylitol

2 TBSP lemon juice

1 tsp. vegetable glycerin

½ oz. / 15g butter

1 tsp. rum

¾ tsp. ground cinnamon

¼ tsp. ground nutmeg

pinch ground clove

Core and roughly chop the apples. Leave the skins on. Skins are awesome!

Place the apples in a pan over medium heat with the xylitol, lemon juice, and glycerin, and cook until the apples are very soft – about 15 minutes.

Carefully pour the apples into a blender and blend until very smooth.

Add the butter, rum, cinnamon, nutmeg, and clove and blend until completely blended.

Pour into an airtight container and store in the fridge until ready to layer with freshly churned Apple Pie a la Mode Ice Cream – page 82.

Sour Cherry Chunks

8 oz. / 225g sour cherries (canned), very well drained

1 TBSP xylitol

1 TBSP vegetable glycerin

Tip the well-drained cherries onto several sheets of kitchen paper and blot them to remove as much excess juice as possible.

Place the cherries in a small pan with the xylitol and glycerin, stir well, and heat gently until just warm. Remove from the heat, stir well, and leave the cherries to soak until cold. Pour the cherries into an airtight container and store in the fridge.

An hour before you are ready to layer the cherries into freshly churned Double Cherry Choc Chunk Ice Cream – page 76 – pour the cherries into a sieve and leave them to drain so that they are not dripping with juice when you layer them into your ice cream.

Lemon Curd (*uses eggs)

4 eggs

7 oz. / 200g xylitol

⅓ cup / 2 ½ fl oz. lemon juice (approx. 2 lemons)

Zest of 1 lemon

4 oz. / 110g coconut oil, melted

4 oz. / 110g butter, melted

Whisk the eggs well with a fork and pour into a small pan.

Add the xylitol, lemon juice, lemon zest, coconut oil, and butter. Whisk ingredients together well.

Place on the stove over a medium heat and STIR CONSTANTLY as the mixture slowly thickens. It takes 12 – 15 minutes to thicken fully. Embrace it. Be patient.

DO NOT ALLOW THE MIXTURE TO BOIL – it will curdle, or you will get scrambled eggs.

When the mixture is thick enough to coat the back of a spoon, quickly remove it from the heat and pour it through a fine mesh sieve into a glass, lidded container (such as a Pyrex storage bowl). No, you cannot omit this step. It must be sieved!

Stir the mixture in the sieve until you are left with only the zest pulp and a few strands of egg. Use a second, clean spatula to scrape the underside of the sieve as you go.

Once all the curd has been passed through the sieve, leave uncovered until completely cold, stirring every 10 minutes to prevent a skin from forming.

When cold, put the lid on the container and place in the 'fridge. Once chilled it will be thick and spreadable.

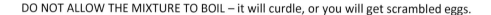

Afraid of making egg custards? Don't be! I used to be, but I've discovered that egg custards are easy, beautiful, and making them is downright therapeutic. Egg custards taught me that the fear is always worse than the reality. Me and egg custards are best buds now, and they are the finest excuse I know to stand by the stove and do nothing except gaze lovingly into a saucepan and stir the contents. These days, when I need a break from doing, I make something that requires an egg custard; just so I can stand still for 12 minutes. Egg custards rock.

In other news, not only are egg custards awesome to make, but this Lemon Curd makes my mouth insanely happy. Tart, sweet, silky smooth. GO, lemons!

Peanut Butter Drops

1 cup / 8 fl oz. smooth peanut butter, unsweetened

1 TBSP glycerin

1 oz. coconut flour

4 tsp. konjac flour / glucomannan powder

Leave the jar of peanut butter at room temperature overnight so that it softens. Put the peanut butter in a bowl with the glycerin and mix well.

Sieve the coconut flour and konjac flour together into a separate bowl and mix well.

Add the mixed flours into the peanut butter in 4 batches, mixing well after each addition.

When all the flours are well incorporated, cover and place in the 'fridge until the peanut butter stiffens.

Line a flat plate with plastic wrap, and pull small pieces of peanut butter out of the bowl and place on the plate. Once all the peanut butter has been divided into little pieces, place the peanut butter drops in the freezer on the plate.

Once frozen, if you are storing the peanut butter balls for any length of time before adding them to your ice cream, remove from the plate and place in a glass, airtight container, using greaseproof paper between the layers.

~~~~~~

Sneaky peanut butter tip: if you buy peanut butter freshly made from a store that has a peanut butter grinder, you may need to add more coconut and konjac flours to this recipe as this kind of peanut butter tends to be softer than peanut butter in a jar. I used Trader Joe's Smooth Peanut Butter in this recipe. Make sure to check the label if you buy pre-packaged peanut butter. The only ingredients should be peanuts and salt.

Caramel Toasted Pine Nuts

1 TBSP xylitol

1 TBSP heavy cream (see page 12)

1 TBSP butter

2 tsp. caramel extract

2 ½ oz. / 70g pine nuts, toasted

Place the xylitol, cream, butter, and caramel extract in a pan over medium heat and bring just to the boil. Add the pine nuts, lower the heat and simmer for about 5 minutes, stirring often, until the pine nuts are golden brown and the cream mixture has become caramelly.

Turn the nuts onto parchment or wax paper on a cookie tray or similar, and spread them until they only one layer of nuts deep. Leave to cool.

After 30 minutes, stir the nuts around well and then spread them out as before. The stirring is important, as it will cause the caramel to crystallize and stop them from being sticky. Then, once they're completely cold they will be dry and no longer clump together.

Once the nuts are cool, stir them around well and spread them out for a third time.

When the nuts are completely cold, spoon them into an airtight container and keep them in the fridge until you want to mix them into freshly churned Lavender Surprise Ice Cream – page 38.

~~~~~~

Chocolate Dipped Macadamia Nuts

Line a ¼ baking sheet or something similar with parchment paper.

Barely warm the Chocolate Fudge Ripple (page 87) until it is just fluid. Using a dipping fork (see resources page 27) – or a regular fork if that's what you have – toss each macadamia nut into the ripple and then fish out with your fork. Tap the fork handle on the edge of the container to shake the excess ripple off and then gently flip or roll it from the fork onto the parchment paper.

When all the nuts are dipped, place them in the freezer for at least 2 hours. Once the ripple has firmed up, layer the nuts with parchment paper in an air-tight container. Return to the freezer until you need to add them to a freshly churned batch of Ballistic Coffee Ice Cream – page 44.

You can add as many chocolate dipped macadamias to your Ballistic Ice Cream as you want, so I did not give you a quantity. Have at it!

Chocolate Chunks

8 oz. / 225g butter

1 oz. / 30g glycerin

1 ½ oz. / 40g powdered xylitol (see page 13) (NO substitutes!)

3 oz. / 85g 100% unsweetened chocolate, chopped

Put the butter, glycerin, and powdered xylitol in a pan over medium-low heat until the butter melts.

Stir well until the xylitol is completely dissolved.

Turn the heat to very low and add the chopped 100% chocolate. Stir continuously until the chocolate has melted and the mixture is completely smooth.

Line a dish, ¼ sheet baking pan or something similar with parchment paper. The smaller the dish or tray the thicker your chunks will be, so choose accordingly.

Pour the chocolate butter onto the parchment paper.

Carry the dish or tray carefully to the freezer, place on a level surface inside, and freeze them for at least two hours.

Once frozen, remove from the freezer, peel off the parchment paper and place on a cutting board.

Working quickly, and touching the chocolate as little as possible with your fingers (because melty), cut the slab into chunks the size you want in your ice cream. You do you.

Place the chunks in an air-tight container and store in the freezer until your ice cream has churned.

~~~~~~

They're intensely chocolatey!

They're incredibly smooth!

They're not hard to bite into when frozen!

They're easy to make!

All in all...they're awesome!

Perfect KETO chocolate chunks to stir into your ice cream!

Sugar-free Marshmallows

¼ cup / 2 fl oz. cold water

1 TBSP powdered gelatin

5 ¼ oz. / 150g xylitol (NO substitutes!)

¼ cup / 2 fl oz. hot water

¼ cup / 2 fl oz. vegetable glycerin

1 tsp. vanilla extract

Powdered xylitol

Spray a cookie tray with coconut oil spray and set aside.

Put the cold water in a small dish and sprinkle the powdered gelatin slowly and evenly over the surface so that it dissolves in the water. Set aside.

Place the xylitol, hot water, and vegetable glycerin in a small pan over a high heat.

The xylitol will melt and become clear.

Gently add the softened gelatin to the pan and stir carefully until it has dissolved.

Once the gelatin has dissolved, allow the syrup to come to the boil.

CAUTION! MELTED XYLITOL IS RIDICULOUSLY HOT. Don't be scared, but PLEASE BE CAREFUL. (The boiling point of water is 100 °C. The boiling point of xylitol is 212 °C. That's hot.)

Carefully, and slowly to avoid splashes, pour the boiling syrup into a large glass mixing bowl, or the bowl of your stand mixer, if you have one.

Add the vanilla extract, and then whisk on HIGH – either in your stand mixer or with a hand mixer – for 15 minutes. Yes, 15 minutes. If you use a hand mixer you will start to hate me at about the 4 ½ minute mark because it will feel like 15 minutes already and you still have 10 ½ to go.

As you whisk, the syrup will transform into a white, fluffy meringue-like mass. After 15 minutes you will get stiff peaks, like meringue.

Transfer the marshmallow into a piping bag with a small plain nozzle in it. Pipe small blobs of marshmallow onto the cookie trays sprayed with coconut oil.

Lightly sieve powdered xylitol over the marshmallows, and leave to set for several hours. Store in an airtight glass container using greaseproof or waxed paper between the layers.

Note: This recipe makes enough for one batch of mix-ins and one batch of Chocolate Fudge Ripple.

Sugar-free Meringue Cookies (*uses eggs)

3 fresh egg whites (pasteurized whites will not whip)

½ TBSP lemon juice

5 oz. / 140 g xylitol (NO substitutes!)

Pre-heat oven to 225F.

Place the egg whites in a large mixing bowl, add the lemon juice and whisk using either a stand- or hand-mixer until the egg whites have formed stiff, dry peaks.

Add the xylitol, a tablespoon at a time, whisking very well between each addition.

Once you have added the last of the xylitol, continue whisking until the meringue is stiff and very glossy.

Using a piping bag with the nozzle of your choice, fill the bag with meringue and pipe small shapes onto a baking tray lined with parchment paper.

Place the baking sheet(s) in the center of the pre-heated oven and bake for 2 hours.

After 2 hours, turn the oven off and leave the meringues in the warm oven overnight.

If the meringues are still sticky in the morning, leave them in the oven until they are dry, or if you need the oven, place them somewhere dry until they are ready. This could take up to 2 days. Patience is a virtue.

~~~~~~

Sneaky go-faster tip: if you don't have the time – or the inclination – for all that waiting, but you really, really want to make Lemon Meringue Pie Ice Cream, use sugar-free marshmallows instead (recipe on page 94). You will have soft white bits instead of crunchy white bits, but the taste will be very similar.

If you want more sugar-less meringue-making tips: head over to www.carriebrown.com, click on the recipes link, and type 'Meringue Cookies' in the search box.

~~~~~~

To me, this recipe is the ultimate giving-the-finger to sugar. Oh my. Did I really just type that out loud? But really, it's true. What is meringue except a bit of egg white holding a whole ton of sugar in suspension? Well now you can have your meringues, and eat them too. I must admit, it still feels incredibly naughty eating sugar-less meringues, even though it isn't. Take THAT, sugar!

Shortbread Cookies – plain / lemon / cinnamon

7 oz. / 200g almond flour (ground almonds)

1 oz. / 30g finely ground chia seeds (white chia looks prettier, but black works fine)

2½ oz. / 70g xylitol

1 tsp. xanthan gum

3 oz. / 85g cold butter

Put the almond flour, ground chia seeds, xylitol, and xanthan gum** in a food processor and pulse a couple of times to mix well.

Cut the butter into small squares and add to the dry ingredients in the processor.

Pulse until it resembles fine breadcrumbs – about 15 pulses. Pulse a couple more times and it will start to ball together.

Turn out onto a work surface and lightly knead to form a soft dough and roll into a sausage shape about 1.5" in diameter. Use a serrated edge knife to slice the dough sausage into ¼" thick slices.

Place the slices on a baking sheet sprayed with coconut or avocado oil, and bake in the center of the oven at 300F, for 20 – 23 minutes until they are golden brown.

Remove from the oven and leave to cool on the baking sheet. Step away from the cookies!

Once cool, move the cookies to a cooking rack and leave until completely cold.

Pack in an airtight container and leave overnight if you can possibly manage it, before you eat them. I know, I know. Trust me, they are better if left.

Break them into pieces (whatever size you like in your ice cream) and place in the freezer before churning so that they are frozen prior to adding to the freshly churned ice cream.

~~~~~~

**For Lemon Shortbread: add the zest of 2 lemons to the dry ingredients in the food processor and then follow recipe as written.

**For Cinnamon Shortbread: add 1 tsp. ground cinnamon to the dry ingredients in the food processor and then follow recipe as written.

These babies can be thrown together in a New York minute. What's not to love? You won't want to put a whole batch in one churn of ice cream, so dunk a few in your morning cuppa!

Walnut Cookies

2 ½ oz. / 70g walnuts

2 oz. / 55g almond flour (ground almonds)

1 oz. / 30g finely ground chia seeds (white chia looks prettier, but black works fine)

1 ¼ oz. / 35g xylitol

½ tsp. xanthan gum

1 ½ oz. / 40g cold butter

½ tsp. vanilla extract

Put the walnuts in a food processor and pulse until you have walnut meal. Be careful not to process too long and end up with walnut butter!

Add the almond flour, ground chia seeds, xylitol, and xanthan gum to the walnuts in the food processer and pulse a couple of times to mix well.

Cut the butter into small squares and add with the vanilla extract to the dry ingredients in the processor.

Pulse until it resembles fine breadcrumbs – about 15 pulses. Pulse a couple more times and it will start to ball together.

Turn out onto a work surface and lightly knead to form a soft dough and roll into a sausage shape about 1.5" in diameter. Use a serrated edge knife to slice the dough sausage into slices.

Place the slices on a baking sheet sprayed with coconut or avocado oil, and bake in the center of the oven at 300F, for 20 – 23 minutes until they are golden brown.

Remove from the oven and leave to cool on the baking sheet. Step away from the cookies!

Once cool, move the cookies to a cooking rack and leave until completely cold.

Pack in an airtight container and leave overnight if you can possibly manage it, before you eat them. I know, I know. Trust me, they are better if left.

Break them into pieces (whatever size you like in your ice cream) and place in the freezer before churning so that they are frozen prior to adding to the freshly churned ice cream.

~~~~~~

Walnuts tend to be oily so work as quickly as you can, and chill your hands under cold running water before you start trying to handle it.

This should be about the right amount for one batch of Banana Cream Pie Ice Cream, but I won't tell if you snaffle a couple before they get frozen. What happens in this book, stays in this book.

Chocolate Fudge Brownies (*uses eggs)

2 TBSP butter

2 eggs

1 tsp. vanilla extract

3 TBSP cocoa powder

3 TBSP powdered xylitol (see page 13)

Melt the butter in a pan, or in a bowl in the microwave. Remove from the heat. Add the eggs and vanilla extract and whisk well.

Sieve the cocoa powder and powdered xylitol directly into the pan or bowl and stir well until batter is completely mixed.

Pour the batter evenly into 30 mini muffin tins, or use 30 mini muffin paper cases on a baking sheet. You can also use a silicone candy mold if you have such a thing floating around (see resources on page 27). The goal is thin(ish) discs of fudge brownie so that you don't need to do a lot of work afterwards to get them into bite-sized pieces for the ice cream.

Bake at 350 F for 10 – 12 minutes until they are firm and springy to the touch. Leave to get completely cold then store in an airtight container in the freezer until ready to layer them with freshly churned ice cream.

~~~~~~

Chocolate Cheesecake Crust

5 oz. / 140g butter

4 oz. / 110g erythritol

8 oz. / 225g almond flour (ground almonds)

2 oz. / 55g cocoa powder, sifted

Prepare your cheesecake pan by lining with parchment paper, which will make removal easier. I used a square one as that is a breeze to cut and portion, but you can use whatever tin you like. I recommend using a loose-bottomed or spring-form pan as these make it a lot easier to get your masterpiece out without spoiling the crust or sides.

Melt the butter in a small pan on the stove, or a bowl in the microwave.

Add the erythritol, almond flour, and sifted cocoa powder and mix until completely combined.

Press the crust in the bottom of your prepared pan, cover the crust with parchment paper, and freeze until the Mocha Cocoa Fudge Cheesecake is churned and ready to freeze – page 60.

KETOVANGELIST KITCHEN RESOURCES

WEBSITE : www.ketovangelistkitchen.com

PODCAST : www.ketovangelistkitchen.com/category/podcast

FACEBOOK GROUP : www.facebook.com/groups/ketovangelistkitchen

TWITTER : www.twitter.com/KetovanKitchen

PINTEREST : www.pinterest.com/KetovanKitchen

INSTAGRAM : www.instagram.com/ketovangelistkitchen

KETOVANGELIST GENERAL KETO RESOURCES

WEBSITE : www.ketovangelistkitchen.com

PODCAST : www.ketovangelist.com/category/podcast/

FACEBOOK GROUP : www.facebook.com/groups/theketogenicathlete/

KETOGENIC ATHLETE RESOURCES

WEBSITE : www.theketogenicathlete.com

PODCAST : www.theketogenicathlete.com/category/podcast/

FACEBOOK GROUP : www.facebook.com/groups/theketogenicathlete/

WHERE TO FIND ME

www.CarrieBrown.com : delicious recipes for optimal nutrition, wellness, & fat-loss, with tips & tricks for living a super healthy, sane life, as well as travel & things to make you think.

PODCAST : www.ketovangelistkitchen.com/category/podcast

FACEBOOK (page) : www.facebook.com/CarrieBrownBlog

FACEBOOK (personal) : www.facebook.com/flamingavocado

TWITTER : www.twitter.com/CarrieBrownBlog

PINTEREST : www.pinterest.com/CarrieBrownBlog

INSTAGRAM
@carrieontrippin : day-to-day moments captured with my iPhone
@biggirlcamera : road trips, landscapes, flowers, fences, barns, & whatever else grabs my attention captured with my Big Girl Camera
@lifeinthesanelane : food, recipes, inspiration, and sane living tips
@mistermchenry : The world according to Mr. McHenry

FLICKR : www.flickr.com/photos/carrieontrippin

MEDIUM : www.medium.com/@CarrieBrownBlog : random musings on life, the Universe, & everything. Possibly rantier, more sensitive, & more controversial.

COOKBOOKS

E-cookbook / pdf versions : www.carriebrown.com/archives/31768

Print versions : www.amazon.com/author/browncarrie

I am an author, podcast co-host, recipe developer, & photographer, creating useful, fun, & beautiful stuff about food, travel, and living a sane life.

I am a British American ex-professional pastry chef with a crazy, 4-country, 3-continent-spanning resume including a chocolate TV show, a chocolate cookbook, & making pastries for the Queen of England. I trained at the National Bakery School in London.

I now use my pastry-cheffing talents to create scrumptious recipes to help the world eat smarter, live better, & put the 'healthy' back into healthy again. I create gluten-free, grain-free, sugar-free recipes for KETO, LCHF, SANE, LowCarb, Paleo, Primal, WheatBelly, Wild Diet, & other health-focused, whole-food dietary approaches.

This cookbook joins "The KETO Crockpot", "Eat Smarter! Holidays", "Eat Smarter! Smoothies and Sides", "Eat Smarter! Soups", & "Drink Smarter! Beverages" on the culinary bookshelf. All jammed with serious whole food goodness & YUM.

When I am not making stuff up in the kitchen you'll likely find me roaring around the country shooting landscapes & otherwise exploring this amazing world that we live in. I like life better when it's real, rambunctious, & slightly irreverent.

I have a humongous appetite, an accent like crack (apparently), & a love for people who keep on going when the going gets tough. I think leeks are the finest vegetables on earth. I can't swim.

I love living in Seattle with a couple of large cameras, a ridiculous amount of cocoa powder, a far infra-red sauna, & a pile of cats – Florence, Zebedee, Daisy, & Mr. McHenry. We're incredibly grateful for all that living here affords us. We love it here!

Connect with us on social media: we'd love to meet you!

Ice Creams - KETO

Ice Creams – Low Carb High Fat

Mix-ins

51919560R00064

Made in the USA
San Bernardino, CA
07 August 2017